Fatherless No More shows us the miraculous difference our heavenly Father makes in a fatherless life. The love of God fills empty spaces and heals broken hearts!

—CeCe Winans
Grammy and Dove
Award-Winning Gospel Singer

Through the story of his life, Tim Johnson discovers his heavenly Father and realizes that without Him we are all fatherless. As my personal pastor and mentor, Tim has taught me that the answer to whatever my heavenly Father asks is yes—even before He asks! This posture before the Lord opens up the floodgates of heaven.

—Jon Phelps
Founder, Cochairman, and
CEO, Full Sail University

Fatherless No More seemed like less of a book to read and more of an impartation to receive. There is an impartation of hope, strength, and faith. There is a revelation of God's love and intentionality in spite of life and in light of life's circumstances. I believe this book is going to bring understanding and birth forgiveness, healing, deliverance, and transformation for many.

—Tina Campbell
Multiple Grammy Award-Winning
Gospel Singer and Songwriter

The profound existential dilemmas of meaning and purpose are very well framed by the question "Whom do I belong to?" Pastor Tim Johnson has written a very helpful book chronicling his journey from fatherless to fatherless no more. He has woven out of his story and walked with God a valuable path for others to follow. I found his articulation of the Five A's a very useful way to provide a personal application of his story for each reader.

—MICHAEL ZODA, PHD
MARRIAGE AND FAMILY THERAPIST

This moving and courageous memoir is a testament to the strength of the human spirit and the life-changing impact of finding one's true Father. Pastor Tim opens his heart through vivid storytelling of raw realities, resilience, faith, and the journey of pain to purpose, while discovering God's love. His words offer a universal message of hope, healing, and belonging that resonates with anyone seeking to understand their worth and purpose. *Fatherless No More* is a must-read for those feeling lost, reminding us all that we are never truly alone.

—JAIR CLARKE
FORMER CTO, MICROSOFT;
PUBLIC COMPANY BOARD MEMBER

Tim Johnson writes a compelling journal about his growing up in Sarasota, Florida, without an earthly father. He called his condition "fatherlessness." His condition is like many young men's today growing up without an earthly father. Tim often had the feelings of an orphan. The Holy Spirit would intercede for his heavenly Father when he needed help at pivotal junctions in his personal life's journey. He soon became aware that it was the Holy Spirit speaking to him as his heavenly Father. The Holy Spirit would get his attention often in situations when he needed help in charting his course. Tim's relationship with the heavenly Father has helped guide him on a journey that has been filled with successes. He is a pastor who gets great joy leading people to the Father.

When I was coaching in the NFL and working as a scout for the Steelers, I witnessed many young men who could benefit by reading Tim's book. His account of a maturing young life is a strong message for men and women. He recounts situations that are not uncommon to some of their experiences. The conversations he had with his heavenly Father strengthen his character and his direction on his journey. Reading Tim's book will tug at your heart and mind. You will learn that life is good when you know the heavenly Father. This book would be the best investment you could make.

—JOE GREENE
FOUR-TIME SUPER BOWL CHAMPION (IX, X, XIII, XIV); NFL HALL OF FAME INDUCTEE (1987); NFL DEFENSIVE PLAYER OF THE YEAR (1972 AND 1974); ROOKIE OF THE YEAR (1969); TEN-TIME NFL ALL-PRO SELECTION

Fatherless No More is the recounting of a man's life who, while being wonderfully raised by his devoted mother, grew up with a deep insufficiency: his dad was absent. Pastor Tim Johnson's journey to finding the love of the Father will inspire all who need more than any man can give.

—Brett Fuller
Bishop, Grace Covenant Churches
of Washington, DC; Co-chaplain,
Washington Commanders

Tim Johnson is an exceptional man with an exceptional story. You will be inspired by this book to let go of every excuse for not believing you can find a way to live an extraordinary life, regardless of your obstacles, struggles, and limitations.

—Rice Broocks
Cofounder, Every Nation Ministries;
Best-Selling Author, *God's Not Dead*

Fatherless No More is an amazing story of God rescuing a fatherless boy, giving him a new life, and turning him into a great father. I believe Tim Johnson's book will help fatherless boys find their heavenly Father and help all men who read it to become better fathers.

—Professor Jack Deere, ThD

Powerful! Whether the stories will have you laughing, crying, or at times truly inspired, the teachings from these pages will equip you to be that someone God the Father destined for you to become. But before engaging in this book, go look in the mirror. You're about to encounter love from the heavenly Father that will free you in a way you no longer recognize the old you. May the Spirit guide you. Thank you, Jesus!

—D. J. DOZIER
PRESIDENT AND CEO, D2D; LEAD PRINCIPAL
CONSULTANT, SPORTS INNOVATION X; AUTHOR,
DECIDE TO DOMINATE; FORMER TWO-
SPORT PROFESSIONAL ATHLETE; FORMER
ALL-AMERICAN, PENN STATE FOOTBALL

Fatherlessness has become a huge problem in America today. The absence of men leading our homes is having a dramatic impact on families. In *Fatherless No More*, Tim Johnson not only gives us an up-close-and-personal look at the challenges of growing up without a father; he gives solutions to the problem, which are grounded in a relationship with Jesus Christ.

—TONY DUNGY
FORMER NFL COACH; NATIONAL
SPOKESMAN, ALL PRO DAD

FATHERLESS
NO MORE

Foreword by Joe Gibbs

TIM JOHNSON

WITH MAX DAVIS

FATHERLESS

UNDERSTANDING WHO WE ARE WHEN
WE KNOW WHO THE FATHER IS

NO MORE

Fatherless No More by Tim Johnson
Published by Harp & Sword Media
129 S Main St #260
Grapevine, TX 76051

Cover Design by Joe DeLeon of DeLeon Design
Interior Design by Will Rainier

International Standard Book Number: 979-8-9894441-8-2
Ebook ISBN: 979-8-9894441-9-9

Printed in the United States of America

This book is dedicated to my momma because there's nobody like her in this world.

Ma, thank you is an understatement for all that you did for us. When you didn't think anyone was looking, I saw the selfless love and sacrifices you made. For that I want to say thank you!

I love you now and forever.

CONTENTS

PART II: YOUR PATHWAY TO FREEDOM

FOREWORD

I will never forget one of my earliest experiences with Tim.

It was shortly after he joined our football team in Washington. We always held a chapel service the night before our games for anyone associated with our team who had an interest in attending. When we played on the road, we would often invite someone from the city we were playing in to lead the service.

On one occasion the chaplain we had lined up to speak fell ill earlier in the day and had to cancel at the last minute. I remember multiple people coming to me, recommending that Tim lead the service. While I still did not know Tim well or his passion for the Lord at that time, I trusted those around me and asked Tim if he would lead chapel that night.

I'm sure glad I did.

Tim's testimony left an impact on me and everyone in that room that night, and his love for the Lord was evident.

Since that time, I have been blessed to get to know Tim on a deeper level—first as a player, where he quickly emerged as one of our key leaders and helped us win Super Bowl XXVI. Eventually Tim's playing career would come to an end—but his desire to share the love of Jesus never did. He shifted. Currently he serves as the senior pastor of Orlando World Outreach Church, with a goal of reaching the people of

Orlando and connecting them to God and one another while equipping them to serve their local community.

Tim and I also have a passion for sharing our faith with the incarcerated through the work of each of our prison and jail outreaches.

In *Fatherless No More*, Tim shares the story of his childhood and growing up without the influence of an earthly father figure. Despite the devoted love of his mother, there were times in his life when he felt a void or even as if he were some kind of mistake. I'm sure many people can relate to feeling that way at various times in their lives.

The great news that Tim shares in this book is that God loves us and has a plan for each of us. I know I really appreciate Tim for sharing his story and for sharing his passion and love for Jesus. And the best news of all? It is something we can all share in.

—Joe Gibbs
National Football League Hall of Fame Coach;
NASCAR Hall of Fame Owner,
Joe Gibbs Racing

PART I

FROM FATHERLESS TO *THE* FATHER

CHAPTER 1

AN EMPTY PICTURE FRAME

We loved Butch but were afraid of him at the same time. When I say "afraid," I'm not talking about being nervous over some looming harsh disciplinary action, as if he might pop us with his belt or something. I'm talking he's-going-to-kill-you afraid. Whenever Butch came home in the evenings after drinking and was out of his mind with rage, he'd scream and rant, yelling profanities while threatening to beat up or kill my grandmother. My uncle once went to using his fists on Butch because he was convinced Butch had molested his sister.

Butch wasn't a small fellow, either. He had worked the fields all his life, so he could be quite an intimidating character when he wanted to be, especially to a young boy. In the little bit of backyard there was, he had these cages with animals. It was like a mini farm with rabbits and chickens, and he would eat them. When he wanted a chicken or rabbit, he'd pick one out, wring its neck, skin it, and then tear the animal apart. And that could be a little intimidating for a young boy. I remember trembling, with no other man around to protect me, as Butch stomped through the house, ranting and raving. But truth be told, I was more scared for my grandmother than for myself. The hostility of whatever Butch had been through in his life, the pain oozing from his festering wounds, would be unleashed on her, not us kids—my two brothers, Don and

Mike, and me. What's heart-wrenching is when Butch was sober, he was a pretty decent guy. He'd take us kids to Burger King for Whoppers and let us get ice cream cones or whatever we wanted. That was the big treat of the week, but then, when Friday night hit, it was like terror. Whenever Butch came home in the evening after drinking, I remember him being loud and profanity spewing every which way, combined with the threats that he was going to kill my grandmother. Like I said, we loved Butch. Then, he'd go crazy. It kept my young mind in a state of confusion because I never knew which Butch was going to show up. Mostly, though, the thought of him hurting my grandmother broke my heart, and it was going to be a problem if he ever did. We had a special bond.

What's amazing is through all of Butch's troubling emotions, my grandmother would stay as cool as a cucumber on ice, which always baffled me. She was our rock. She used to sew and make clothes and pillows and fix couches and all kinds of things. Sewing was her deal, her escape. Butch would be shaking up the little house with his threats, and Grandma would just sit at her sewing machine, humming and stitching away, not budging an inch. It was as if she had become completely numb to it all. Not me. I felt every threat, heard every vulgarity, smelled the stench of alcohol on his clothes.

As you may have guessed, Butch was my grandfather. Actually, he was my step-grandfather, if you want to call him that. My biological grandfather was nowhere to be found, and Butch was married to my grandmother. I'm not excusing his explosive behavior, but at least he showed up and on his good days acted as though he cared a little bit. I wish I would have had a chance to see Butch before he died. That's the one regret I have about my relationship with him. After knowing the salvation of Jesus, I wish I had had a chance to see Butch. If he was right here, I would say: "Butch, I appreciate everything you did. I appreciate the way you protected us as kids. I appreciate the opportunity you gave us to have experiences we wouldn't have had because we didn't have a lot of money. We saw and learned a lot about animals, even though they didn't live long because they became food. I know you must have had a lot of pain in your life because of the pain that I saw you cause my grandmother in your shouts, screams, profanity, and drunkenness, and all those things. There was something that was right in the midst of so much wrong, and that was your heart wanting to take care of us. I think it was a picture of what God wanted for you. He wants you to know that He sent Jesus to take care of you. The way Jesus came to take care of you is He came, in human form, to live the life you couldn't live. Then He died the death that you deserved, in your place for your sin, for all the pain. Three days later He rose from the dead to forgive you for all your sins and give you a whole new life, free from the pain of your past. If you trust Him, He'll come into your heart, and He'll never leave. Butch, would you like a chance to experience new life? Because I would love to pray with you." That would be the scenario I would have loved to have in a one-on-one meeting with Butch, after he'd done so much for us, to offer him the gift of eternal life. That's what I wish. But this is a book about fatherlessness, not grandfatherlessness, or step-grandfatherlessness, right? Absolutely. Keep reading.

During that time, my mother was young and quite stunning. She had exquisite long hair and one of the best figures in Sarasota. Men would see her and melt. The problem was she was looking for love, as the song goes, in the wrong places. Coming out of abuse where she was devalued, Mom didn't know her identity as a beloved daughter of the Father. As a result, she let men take advantage of her and sometimes have their way, especially if they showed her affection, which was really not love at all but a cheap imitation. And the pain cut deep when these guys were unfaithful. The Lord, however, would relentlessly pursue her, chase her down with His outrageous love, and rescue her out of the dark pit she was trapped in.

Before that revelation of divine love and grace, however, she had a one-night stand under the steamy Florida moonlight nearly sixty years ago with a guy she worked at the cafeteria with. Boom, just like that, I was conceived. Nine months later, at 2:31 a.m. January 29, 1965, Sarasota Memorial Hospital welcomed a baby boy into this world. To Mom's credit, she knew there was a little human growing inside her womb, and she loved me from the moment she found out. There has never been a doubt that my mother loved me.

Tired and run down a lot, she was a hard worker, juggling two, sometimes three, jobs at the same time. Because she couldn't afford her own place, we lived with my grandmother and Butch for a few years. In the beginning it was six of us in a small house on the lower-income end of Sarasota, Florida, on 21st Street. Most of the time it was my mom, my two brothers, Grandma, Butch, and me. Later on, a sister and another brother would be added from different fathers. Mom was carrying a heavy load of guilt and shame but felt powerless to stop the cycle. The men just used her, and she allowed them to.

It was a highly dysfunctional situation, yet in the end my mother would become a testimony to how the Father can step into the most hopeless of situations and transform someone with His grace. Down the line, He would send her a godly husband, though I would be long gone by then.

A few days after Mom brought me home from the hospital to Butch and Grandmother's house, there was a knock at the front door. Mom must have been at work. My grandmother answered while she had me coddled in her arms, patting me, swaying back and forth like grandmothers do. When she opened the door, my father was standing there. I don't know whether he was in shock or what, but he looked me over good and hard, eyed my grandmother, and then turned around and walked away. Another account says he may have picked me up, took me for a bit, and then dropped me back off and left for good. Either way, that was it. If there would ever even be a record of my recollection of years, it would be of me just being left, abandoned with no explanation. He just disappeared. Never came back. Never showed up. Never sent presents at Christmas or on birthdays. Never came to a ball game or a graduation.

On my birth certificate there's a blank space where my father's name was supposed to go. It was never filled in. Worse, there was a blank space in my soul that would remain unfilled for the next two decades.

Then, fifty-three years after my birth, I would have a conversation with a fifty-year-old man who had my earthly father's name. In the conversation I found out my father didn't die until 2007. That meant he was alive all those years when I was growing up, without ever seeking me out. The revelation sucker punched me in the pit of my stomach. Even as a middle-aged man, it hurt, really hurt. Thankfully, I was spared emotional wreckage because some years earlier I had come to know the love of *the* Father, who created me for Himself, which is what this book is ultimately about.

Psychologists say the first five to eight years of a child's life are the most formative. For me, growing up without a father was like carrying around an empty picture frame. Because I had no idea what a father, or a husband, or a real man was supposed to look like, whatever mental snapshot I had at the moment of manhood went in that frame. Meanwhile, the screen door to the little cramped house on 21st Street would slam, and Butch would come fuming through. He became the primary picture in my frame for those formative years. With virtually zero technology in those days, my exposure was primarily Butch and the men my mom was bringing to the house. Not many winning snapshots from those. My brother's fathers would come into the picture occasionally, at the very least to visit, and then they would disappear. I didn't even get any of that occasional affection either.

THANKFULLY, I WAS SPARED EMOTIONAL WRECKAGE BECAUSE SOME YEARS EARLIER I HAD COME TO KNOW THE LOVE OF THE FATHER, WHO CREATED ME FOR HIMSELF, WHICH IS WHAT THIS BOOK IS ULTIMATELY ABOUT.

As a fatherless boy I felt unseen, as if I were a mistake, a misfit, and an orphan in my own family. Yet strangely, all those emotions were blurred and churning inside me, simmering. I couldn't put my finger on what was wrong, but it would profoundly impact my behavior and young outlook on life. With no reference point for a healthy, loving father—and all those images going in my picture frame—I wasn't consciously thinking about my fatherlessness. I just knew inherently that something was off, that it wasn't supposed to be this way.

In those early years it was never a question of asking about a father because I didn't know that it was even an option to know about your dad. I was simply left out of the loop as to why I didn't have one. There must have been something lacking in me, I thought. I was the reason. Fatherless boys often feel as though they are a mistake. That was me.

When a person is physically or emotionally abandoned by

their earthly father, the hole in their soul leaves them feeling like an orphan, or homeless, even when surrounded by family. There was no doubt that my mother loved us and worked hard trying to compensate for my father's absence. One of the things she would tell us for many years is, "I'm the mama and the daddy. I take care of you." While she had good intentions and put forth a valiant effort, even disciplining us as though she were the daddy, it fell short, and the images of what a solid man or father looked like were blurry. I thought what was being portrayed before me was it. These were men, and that's how men acted and treated women. As I grew into adolescence, I would begin to repeat that cycle and pattern of disrespect. If you don't know who you are, you don't know how to live. But again, deep inside, I always knew something was off.

CHAPTER 2

SWATTING AT DEMONS

Through a special government program, my mom was finally able to get us a house of our own, which was a major accomplishment and testament to her work ethic to support us. She never wanted to settle on being too dependent on people, even though we were interdependent as a family. Aunties, uncles, everybody chipped in with everything to support one another's families and kids. So having our own place was a huge step. She worked her fingers to the bone at two or three jobs to see it happen. I think my mom was pleased to do what she was doing, taking care of us and making sure we had what we needed. I think there was a joy in that for her. We were not going to be let go of. She had had a very difficult upbringing, and I think she worked against that by working for what she didn't have. Providing she had to "grow up" when she was a little girl, I think she knew how to do it. She was very responsible. Anytime we had a family gathering or a big event on the weekend, she was right in the middle of it, cooking and handling things, and I think she felt a lot of gratification. She felt she was being appreciated. I noticed, over the years, that people talked about my mom's cooking, and that was like a reward. Because she was legit. While we stopped living with my grandmother and Butch, we would still go to their house often because that was the drop-off station for us kids when Mom was working or going out. We needed a place to be and

11

someone to watch over us, and Grandmother always came through with open arms.

Although my overall perception of men was warped—all I knew came from the dysfunction and abuse and immorality I'd been witnessing—family in general was a lifeline for me. I had that deep extended family of uncles, aunts, and cousins. We'd go to their houses, and there'd always be a ton of food and fun. My cousins and I would play games such as hide-and-seek and dodgeball in the street and yard, climb trees, and sometimes just throw rocks at stuff. I especially loved a game called hot butter biscuit, during which one player throws the ball up, and whoever catches it gets tackled and smashed. That was when I began to realize my athletic abilities. I didn't think too much about my fatherlessness when I was playing like that. It was back home, whenever life slowed down and I had time to contemplate things, that I felt I didn't belong, as though something was missing. Though our new house was rarely quiet with us kids running around doing kid things, there were moments that the hollow hole in my soul seemed to echo. People tend to reason that young children don't entertain deep thoughts about life, that they're too busy playing. This is not so. They are listening and observing, picking up on things, even when they are playing. There was so much pain going on around me that no child should be exposed to. The pressure and weight of it all often made me feel like an old soul trapped in a kid's body, even though I often couldn't identify it. That hole inside my soul was shaped like my father, even though most of the time I didn't realize that.

In our new place, we three brothers lived in one room with all our things and no air conditioning. Did I mention we lived in Florida and the summers were hot, Africa hot? Let's just say with three boys occupying the same space, our bedroom was not where any one of us wanted to be for very long because we could barely move around. We slept in a twin bed together and had one dresser and one closet for all three of us. Down the short hallway was a bathroom, my sister, Fleda's room, and Mom's room across from that.

Meanwhile, Mom wasn't getting any better. This was one of the darkest periods of her life, as she was experiencing the fallout from all the toxic relationships. She seemed to be sinking deeper into the pit of despair. She was a tortured soul, looking for identity and love. Unfortunately, the men in her life were incapable of giving her the lasting love and respect she longed for.

One day—I had to have been ten or younger—I wandered out of my room into the hall alone and peered into my mother's room. I don't know what my brothers and sister were doing. They were probably outside playing. Mom's door was open, and what I saw shook me to my young core, leaving me forever changed. She was sitting on the edge of her bed, seemingly lost in another world, while swatting frantically as if she were being assaulted by a swarm of killer bees. She was just swatting at the air, shaking and sobbing. "Get away from me! Get away!" All I could think was, "My mom's going crazy."

I just stood there, frozen in fear, so afraid, so overwhelmed. I felt helpless in that I couldn't do anything to help her—it was as if she was being taken over by demons or something. And I remember a thought shot through my mind: "If something happens to her, what's going to happen to me?" She was the only security I had. No child should have to think these things. I continued to stand there, paralyzed, not knowing how to respond. Entangled in a web of despair, she was being tortured by something. She had always been very in control, worked hard, and kept us together. Now she was just falling apart, right there in front of me. I was confused. I was sad. I was just really trying to figure it out. I'm usually the one who tries to help in different ways. But now I was helpless. I didn't even go in the room. I just stood by the door, listening and watching and wondering, "What's going to happen to us if something happens to her?" It was a very strange, odd, disorienting, confusing experience for me. Mom never noticed me. I later found out she was having a bad reaction to a drug that had unknowingly been slipped into her drink. That is why she never took another drink after that.

At a time when I needed nurturing as a child, my heart ached for my mom. Not being seen even though I was standing right there while she swatted at demons was a snapshot of my life. What stuck in my head from that experience was a feeling of utter helplessness, powerlessness, and fear. She was all I had. There was no loving father around to say, "Son, back up. I got this. I got your mama. I can take care of this." The foundation of who I was had been shaken, and the feeling of vulnerability was something I didn't like. There was no one I could depend on, and at ten years old I had had to figure out a way to protect myself. This need to independently take care of myself became the driving force in my life for the next decade or more.

It didn't help that with our new home, we were now being bused nearly an hour away to a public school in a foreign neighborhood that seemed like a foreign culture. I wish I could say I fully understood, but it always seemed that wherever we were, we were never good enough. We always seemed to be put in a situation where, as minorities, somebody else was controlling our lives. Somebody else was making decisions, and we had no say. I felt vulnerable being that far away from home in a strange place that was predominantly white. It was the first time I'd ever been called "nigger," and I didn't know what to do. I didn't know because no one had ever taught me what to do. Do I fight or walk away or what? Added to my need to take care of myself was a sense of "I have to survive. I have to learn how to adapt to this new environment."

Ironically, looking back, though I was fatherless, *the* Father was already moving and protecting me. I just didn't know it. Years later, while playing in the NFL, I would come to understand that the whole time I had felt like an orphan, He had been there with me. *The* Father, who knew me and loved me before I was formed in my mother's womb, would reveal Himself by pouring His love into my empty soul and embracing me (Jer. 1:5).

Perplexingly, in the midst of those feelings of orphanhood, I had felt different and set apart, as if there was something significant about my life. My emotions were a ball of confusion, but I felt both, not feeling that I was seen, not feeling as if I fit in anywhere, while at the same time sensing that I was a part of something greater, if for no other reason than I was still alive when maybe I should've been dead.

LOOKING BACK, THOUGH I WAS FATHERLESS, THE FATHER WAS ALREADY MOVING AND PROTECTING ME.... YEARS LATER, WHILE PLAYING IN THE NFL, I WOULD COME TO UNDERSTAND THAT THE WHOLE TIME I HAD FELT LIKE AN ORPHAN, HE HAD BEEN THERE WITH ME.

Shortly after I was born, my mother came home from work one day, and my grandmother held me and said, "Emma, you need to take this baby to the hospital. You need to take the baby to the doctor now!" She rushed me to the hospital, where they immediately admitted me because they knew something serious was wrong but didn't know what. They told my mom that there was only a fifty-fifty chance that I would live. It was a Thursday, and Mom said, "I just sat there for hours and hours and hours and cried and cried and cried and cried." A couple of days later she realized she needed to go home and take care of my brothers and some other duties. She reluctantly left the hospital. At home she washed a load of laundry and was in the backyard hanging the clothes on the clothesline to dry, her heart ripping with worry and fear. Now, my grandmother's house was located next to a row of duplexes, not high-rise apartments but a few single-story attached homes. Everything was in close proximity, and my mother and grandmother knew the neighbors.

While my mother was hanging up clothes, she saw a lady whom she'd never seen before sitting on one of the porches. Then, the lady got up and made a beeline over to her. It felt a little strange, as if the woman was on a mission. When she got to Mom, she looked directly at her, eyes piercing, full of love and comfort, and asked, "What are you doing?" It was a strange question because it was obvious what she was doing.

"I'm hanging these clothes out for my baby," Mom replied. "My baby's sick."

Instead of answering, the lady just continued to stand there, gazing at her with tenderheartedness, communicating without speaking. Mom felt a warmth wash over her. Peace filled her heart, and she knew instinctively that her baby boy was going to be fine. At that the lady turned around and walked off. Mom never saw her again, ever. No one could identify her, not even those in the home where she was sitting on the front porch. It was as though she didn't exist. Remember, this is a close, familiar street, with the residents almost like a family. Everyone knew everyone. Right after that the hospital called, and all they said was, "Come get your baby." Mom didn't know what that meant, so then she wondered, "Why? Is he dead?"

At the hospital, the doctor explained that they didn't know what was wrong with me, but whatever it was, I was fine now. After she brought me home, what's really peculiar is Mom never got a bill from the hospital when it should have cost thousands of dollars. Mom is convinced the lady that day was an angel. That's the only description she has because of the mysterious meeting and overwhelming peace she had felt. The lady gave her comfort about me living, that the fifty-fifty prognosis was on the side of life, not death. I was helpless and could do nothing on my own to keep myself alive. The fact that I was still alive felt sovereign to me, felt like God to me, like something is significant about my life, despite still feeling like an orphan.

CHAPTER 3

GOD'S ERASERS

Around that same time, my brothers and I got a chance to play little-league football in the Pop Warner league. It was full speed and full contact, complete with helmets, pads, cleats, and uniforms. Of course, we'd already been playing rough-and-tough unorganized football in the streets and yards, but organized football was a whole new game. We had to learn rules, discipline, hard work, how to function as a team, and to practice, practice, practice when we'd rather be doing something else. It was a lot easier when we could just run around in the yard carefree. At first, all the equipment was awkward, so it took some getting used to. Plus, it was brutally hot, especially with all that gear on. And taking all those hits was tough too. But the payoff was big game days. Yes, with organized ball came a lot of changes—perhaps the most significant that we now had coaches.

Coaches on every level are certainly human, like everyone else, yet a mammoth responsibility has been entrusted to them in that they hold the power to influence lives. I've been privileged to play for some of the greatest of all time: Joe Paterno at Penn State, where we won a national championship; Joe Gibbs with the Washington Redskins, where we won a Super Bowl; Chuck Noll with the Pittsburgh Steelers; and Charlie Cleveland at Sarasota High School, who was a legend in Florida high school football. All those coaches had profound impacts on me, but there was one coach in Pop Warner who I believe it's not a stretch to say was from God.

Another coach, John Patella in Sarasota, appeared on the scene at a critical point in my life and would help shape the trajectory of my path. This man, a fiery Italian, was as tough as nails yet compassionate and motivating. He didn't let me, or anybody, cut corners or make excuses for our situation. He was extremely fair, and at a time when I felt like an orphan in my soul, I couldn't believe this man gave me attention. I remember one time, it was going to be easy to quit. I'd gotten hit exceptionally hard on this particular play, and it shook me up really good. I mean, I was seeing stars. This was quite surprising to me because I didn't understand how you could have all that equipment on and still feel pain. Coach Patella encouraged me to get back up and keep trying. There was something about his voice, something about his presence that made you reach deep within yourself for a piece of courage you didn't know was there. He did it for all of us, but I felt special because sometimes he'd give me a ride home when my mom was working. This thrilled me because there was nothing in me that would ever not want to be wherever he was. His very presence called for my respect. Coach Patella was everything I wished for in a father. He saw potential in me, believed in me, and though it wouldn't necessarily come out in words, I knew he loved me. This was something unusual for me coming from a man. Up to that point, I guess if I had to put the tag of love on a man, surprisingly, it would've been Butch, the provision and treats we got from him, knowing that even in the chaos of his rampages, we wouldn't be harmed.

Our games on Saturdays at Ringling Redskins Park were also kind of like family reunions because so many of my extended family members showed up to watch my brothers, cousins, and me. I can't say I lacked love and support. My uncles would tap me on the shoulder and say, "Go get 'em, Tim. Do good." They cheered us on, along with my sister, who was one of the cheerleaders, dressed in her cheering outfit, waving her pom-poms. Of course, Mom and my aunts were often there. That was another picture of love.

Game days at the park were all-day affairs. We'd go in the morning and not leave till night, after the lights clicked off. Our team would play one game, and that was it. Then, the real fun began because we'd run around from one game to the next, making cup footballs and just continuing to play football unofficially. And it was nine thousand degrees out there, but we didn't care. There was a little-league field and a big-league field, and games were constant all day long. Over time I worked my way up from the little-league field to the big-league field. Regardless of the level you were at, after your game it was a big playground—it was a community. This was our sanctuary right here. This was our safe place that kept us from doing a lot of other stuff. It felt like family. And I had these surrogate fathers because they all enjoyed coming to the games. I felt safe. Though none of them were my father, there was an element of safety that I felt with so many dads. It felt wholesome and hope filled. You had dads out there as volunteer coaches, but then you had dads and uncles who would come to the games as supporters. Because I felt free, I felt covered, and safe. This was the world that felt the most like me. With Coach Patella, it was more that he actually saw me. There was something that made me feel seen. I would do anything to just be there at the practice doing whatever. He made me want to please him and give my all. And we were a pretty good team too. We won championships, and Coach Patella was the foundation for me growing as a young man and seeing more than what I saw in myself.

Men have a responsibility to be a voice and light. It's God's design. Not only *should* men invest in other young men, the next generation, but it is required. It is a requirement for every man to take his place, not just in his family but in this world, starting in their own community. If we don't invest in the next generation, we don't have to worry about our future because we won't have one. I've become the evidence of how real this statement is. Years later, actually only a few years ago, when I was inducted into the Sarasota High School Hall of Fame, Coach Patella was there. He was in his late eighties or nineties, and I was able to make mention of him and the impact he had on my life many years ago to a roomful of people. Now I get to honor him. And when he died, his son called me and said, "Dad wanted you to speak at his celebration of life." So Coach Patella was the beginning of seeing what a man can look like to me as a kid. He became an eraser. I suppressed a lot of the stuff that I had seen and started to focus on the picture of Coach Patella maybe being an example.

IN THE END, IF ALL YOU HAVE IS ALL THOSE ACCOLADES... YOU'VE LOST. YOU WILL LOSE IF YOU DON'T REALIZE IT'S JUST A MOMENT AND IT CAN'T BE YOUR LIFE. THERE IS SOMETHING BIGGER.

In addition, Pop Warner Football gave me a place to feel as though I had a place. Because Coach Patella trained us, he made us good football players, but the love was really the foundation of everything else I experienced. It gave me a sense of accomplishment. A spark had been ignited inside me. I had found my lane to run in. Football gave me a life. It gave me a place to feel like I could be me. I didn't have to try to find a place to fit in, and it helped me escape all the other things I would feel when I wasn't involved.

Biblical scholars and teachers often point out that the Old

Testament is the New Testament concealed, and the New Testament is the Old Testament revealed. Throughout the Old Testament there are shadows and types of Christ and other New Testament truths. While I was growing up in grade school, there were times when our teacher was not present, so we had a substitute teacher who was only a type of the actual teacher. For me, this period of growth, starting with Coach Patella, was like the Old Testament part of my life. The Father was showing me types and shadows of the way He wanted me to follow. The Father wanted to actually reveal to me how much He saw the details, the little things of my life, how He wanted to develop me, and how He wanted me to treat other people.

I think there are two ways to go through life: learning what to do and learning what *not* to do. I've been on both extremes. You've got kids who go through deep, dark, devastating abuse. Those are lessons in what not to do. Living with my father's abandonment, I was learning what not to do. The Father can use those things to help us understand. That's what you're not going to do. Then, He gave me pictures of what to do. So He was carefully guiding me through. And trust me, it wasn't easy at all, in the personal development, the immaturity, the sin, through all the struggles of trying to figure out where in life I belong. Football was a great escape and teacher. It gave me a safe lane to run in, but I couldn't play football twenty-four hours a day, every day of the week. It wasn't the answer for my life. I was still left outside of it grasping. In the end, if all you have is all those accolades, all those wonderful high-lights—if that's all you have, you've lost, as great and as memorable as it will be for the rest of your life. You will lose if you don't realize it's just a moment and it can't be your life. There is something bigger.

CHAPTER 4

THE FATHER FATHERING ME

I was putting on my shoulder pads before one particular practice in the eighth grade, just as I'd done for the previous few years, when I suddenly collapsed to the ground, unconscious. My head hit the concrete so hard that nearly fifty years later I still have a little knot on my skull. When my eyes eventually blinked back open, my mom and other people were standing over me. Then, I blacked out again on the way to the hospital. Once there, it was determined I had suffered an epileptic seizure and almost swallowed my tongue, both of which can be fatal. This was another time I could have very likely been dead, and it seemed there was some greater purpose for me being alive.

The doctor put me on medication and thought playing sports wasn't a good idea for someone with my condition. Upon hearing this, that familiar feeling of helplessness and panic engulfed me. "I can't *not* play sports," I pleaded to my mom. "I *have* to play." Yes, I was a minor, but there was nothing in me that was going to agree with the doctors, even if it cost me. I had nothing else, no other outlet. Football was my place. Mom understood this and reluctantly allowed me to continue playing...but with caution. Thankfully, I played without another incident and was completely off the medication within two years.

What's important to realize, however, is at this particular

time in my life—from seventh to ninth grade in junior high—though football had become my safe place, I was average at best. Sure, I had been pretty good in little league, but there was certainly nothing indicating that I would eventually become a High School All American, a Division I college All American, and an NFL All Pro. My experience with Coach Patella had energized me. He believed in me, saw me, loved me, and pushed me, as he did all the kids, but I had felt it in a special way. And then I hit this bump in the road of being very average in junior high. With Coach Patella pretty much out of the picture, I wasn't anything special to anybody, including myself. Yet football was all I had that kept me going and out of trouble. And believe me, there was plenty of opportunity for trouble. Football gave me an escape, but it wasn't 24/7 and was seasonal. I did try basketball but not for long. That's another story we'll get to in a bit. I was also becoming more independent as a young man, learning to adapt and survive in the situations I found myself in. Survival and self-preservation were driving me. I didn't need anyone except those from the groups I had attached myself to—my teammates and coaches, but mostly my two best buddies. Whenever you saw one of us, you most likely saw all three of us. We stuck together like duct tape and pretty much raised one another. We didn't do the best job, though, because all three of us were orphans—the blind leading the blind, never finding what we were searching for: true home. An orphan is always looking for a home yet can't find it. That was us. Like round pegs in square holes, we felt we never fit in anywhere. So we carved out our own holes to fit in among ourselves.

Still, I zipped up tight that heavy coat of self-protection I'd worn from an early age. Orphans—me included—are very wounded, living out of their woundedness. No one ultimately had my back. I had to man up and take control. The need for a father had been pushed down while I'd efficiently erected mental defenses and survival mechanisms around me. I was strong. I was good. At least I tried to convince myself of it. My circumstances only reinforced my walls.

One day I found myself sitting in the principal's office after being falsely accused. I happened to be with some other guys who had inappropriately touched a girl. I got caught in the same crew, and my name was called. I was scared because I'd never been to the principal's office. Plus, I was way out there in the suburbs at that school almost an hour away from home. Calling my mom was out of the question because she was working one of her three jobs. My reasoning told me there was no way she'd be able to come way out there. That wouldn't even be an option, as it would take her away from earning desperately needed money for us to survive. Our lives were about getting through. There was no cushion to fall back on. Being absent from work for whatever reason meant you didn't get paid. That's why part of me always wanted to be low-maintenance with my mom and to do good for her, because I knew how hard she worked and I had seen so many awful things happen to her with men. I was determined to make my own way. Hard work never scared me. In junior high, I got my first job through the Comprehensive Employment and Training Act (CETA) program for low-income families. I worked in the cafeteria serving the food and doing whatever was needed. It was embarrassing being a student at the school and working in the cafeteria. Junior high kids could be brutal, but I sucked up my pride and did it. I was getting thick-skinned, understanding the reality of where I was from and the needs around my family and wanting to help my mom in every way I could.

So there I was, sitting in the principal's office, and for some reason I was in a room by myself, waiting and not knowing what was going to happen. I remember staring at the cold, formal walls, being very afraid, feeling vulnerable, power-less, and concerned that something serious was about to come down on me. And in that moment, I realized I couldn't call my mom and had no other family member I could call. Most of all, I had no father to call, no man to just get on the phone with and say, "Dad, I don't know what's going on. I didn't do anything wrong. They called me to the office with all these other kids. I'm in the principal's office. Can you come get me? Or can you come up here? I need help." Instead of wanting something that wasn't there, I decided, "I'll just never want that. I'll just never need that." That way I would not have to deal with the disappointment of having nobody to call. "I will figure it out myself. I will figure it out one way or another, or just hope things work out as they should." I had no advo-cate. My life was in that man's hands. I got accused of some-thing someone else did, and I got brought to the office. I just remember sitting in this room by myself like I might as well be in prison.

Thankfully it didn't turn out that way. That situation actu-ally did work out, but it only hardened my resolve to take care of myself. During that period of anger and confusion, it would have been easy for me to drift way off track, to take the bait of false attractions being dangled in front of me. My attitude needed aligning, and the Father would give me a gentle nudge in the right direction.

Back then, to get on a school sports team, you had to try out. If you didn't make it, you were cut, and no participation trophies were handed out. I tried out for the basketball team because my friends tried out, and I made the team. Making the team is pretty good in itself, especially in basketball, because not that many make it. But you have only five starters, and I was the sixth man. That didn't sit well with me because riding the bench wasn't good for my image. It wasn't good enough for who I thought I needed to be on that campus in that small little world. So instead of being a team guy, I quit. The truth is, I would've gotten plenty of playing time. The sixth man usually does and is used for key moments. However, pride and a lack of patience to grow kept me from experiencing that.

There are situations when quitting is justified if you are out of your lane and it is obvious, but my reason for quitting had everything to do with having a bad attitude and wanting to project a certain image. Another time, I had felt rejected and hurt by a girl I liked. The next day I dressed up, over-the-top, to draw attention to myself—I mean, just to be able to satisfy what I was lacking on the inside about my identity. If you rejected me, I was going to come back harder.

I was trying to figure out what I was going to do. Where's my place now? I was not that good at basketball. Football? I was just OK. We had won those championships when I was in little league, but the competition gets increasingly difficult the older you get. I wasn't the biggest, the strongest, or the fastest. All I had was determination. Like most kids, I was all over the place. From the end of ninth grade in junior high to tenth grade in high school was a major transition time, and two seemingly random things happened that appeared to be small, but they had a huge impact on the course of my life path. Just as Coach Patella had been a God thing, these two random acts turned the rudder of my ship.

Looking back, perhaps they weren't random at all.

First, one of the teachers, a white-haired white man, said to me, "Tim, I want you to learn how to sign your autograph. I actually want you to learn because one day people are going to be asking for it." Now, outside looking in, I'm nobody. When I tell you I'm nobody, I mean I was an ordinary black kid from the lower-income part of town in this mostly white middle-class school in the suburbs. Although I would say some people probably saw some raw potential in me, in my own mind I was nobody. And it was the oddest, most awkward moment I was having with a teacher saying, "Sign your autograph." The whole thing was very prophetic. To this day the way I sign my name is the way I learned it back then. That was one of the random things that happened. A shot of hope and possibility was injected that someone, a man, a white man even, saw something in me.

Secondly, I was fifteen and about to go to high school, and I found myself listening, transfixed by a stranger in my own home. A door-to-door salesman in a suit and tie, he sat me down and started explaining to me how my life could be different, how I could be different. It was like having a motivational speaker in my living room. Similar to being taught to sign my autograph, it was bizarre and maybe prophetic. What's crazy is I listened to this man when I didn't always listen to the people who loved me, outside of Coach Patella.

This salesman spoke to me about determination, motivation, discipline, and perseverance. "Determine what you want to do in life, because if you don't, somebody else will," he said. "Motivation is you not waiting for your mama to tell you what you determined to do. You do. You be motivated. You put yourself in that position to actually do what you've determined to do. And discipline is to be willing to do what everybody else won't do." Perseverance is no matter what, never give up.

At that time, I had no goals and wasn't thinking long term about anything. I couldn't see past tomorrow, let alone next year. That's what made it meaningful. What that gentleman said got in my head. The conversation shifted my focus. It changed my life, because that's when I started to actually turn my focus on just one thing: football. I put all my eggs in that basket. He gave me a basic blueprint, and I had to come up with definitions. Instead of being like most young people, ignoring what this adult, who was a stranger, had to say to me, it gripped me. I didn't know him, and there was no reason to listen to him. Yet for some reason, I did. And that man has no clue how he impacted my life. I would love to be able to find him and tell him. When he spoke, something sparked in me that if somebody else sees something in me, I've got to see if it's true. I've got to see if this is real. Perseverance was one of the elements of the blueprint he gave me. I couldn't give up no matter what. Never give up. And I had to work harder than anyone else.

THIS SALESMAN SPOKE TO ME ABOUT DETERMINATION, MOTIVATION, DISCIPLINE, AND PERSEVERANCE. "DETERMINE WHAT YOU WANT TO DO IN LIFE, BECAUSE IF YOU DON'T, SOMEBODY ELSE WILL."

One of the immediate changes I made was I started getting up early in the mornings before school, and I would go in the backyard to work out. I had this old rickety bench and some pieces of iron that looked like railroad tires. And I would lift them. I had no clue what I was doing. I just knew I had to do something. So I went into the backyard, and I would lift weights—those railroad tire pieces of cast iron with holes in them. They don't even make that stuff anymore. I don't even know where we got them. They were just there, almost as if they were waiting for me to find them.

Another thing the mystery salesman told me was, "There's always someone around the corner that's bigger than you, stronger than you, faster than you, and smarter than you." And that's whom I competed with from that point on through my whole high school career. I thought, "Today when I wake up, I'm going to get him." I was competing with this imaginary person he painted in my head who was bigger than me, stronger than me, faster than me. "I'm going to outwork him today," I resolved. I would go back there, lift weights, then go to school. I would come back home, lift weights, and do my homework, then be in bed by nine to ten o'clock. I thought, "I'm going to just see."

As I got a little older, I started meeting people who would actually coach me and teach me—for example, Big Vic would teach me how to lift weights. And I worked out with Scott Truitt my junior year on footwork. And I would just listen to whoever would teach me, outside of actually playing the season. Once the season is over, the training really begins. I was determined and hungry to learn. And that determination included doing my homework and going to bed. I still hung out on the weekends and ran the streets, did all that stuff, but discipline is being willing to do the hard things that most people won't do. And then perseverance was simply just to never quit.

After a while all the hard work started paying off, and I began to develop and separate myself from average. God had given me the ability, and in hindsight I understand how He had been superintending sovereignly over my life all those years, smiling and winking at me, saying, "Son, you belong to Me right now. You don't know it, but you're going to see all these ways that I have guarded you and guided you." The Father was fathering me the whole way.

CHAPTER 5

BAND OF BROTHERS

One conversation with the mysterious man in the suit. That's it. I never saw him again, just as my mom never saw the mysterious lady again. "You can be different," he said. "Here's what you've got to do." For some reason that was bigger than me, I absorbed the words like a sponge and was motivated to take action, and then to follow through, not for days, not for months, but for years. That alone is quite miraculous when you think about it. I went from quitter and average to eventually being All American, All State, Lineman of the Year, and Athlete of the Year at Sarasota High School. I was growing physically and in my new identity.

Yet even with all my development and positive results, I still had that echoing hole shaped like my father inside my soul. As I mentioned, most of the time, I didn't recognize its shape, and I was pushing so hard that I was able to keep myself from thinking about those things. Still, every now and then, such as when I'd see other loving fathers at the games, or when I needed that support only dads can give, those suppressed emotions would start percolating to the surface. My response would be to just slam the lid back down, dig a little deeper inside, and force myself to focus harder on being strong and independent. Mostly, I was functioning in a sports and performance mode, super focused on working the hardest against that imaginary guy that was bigger and faster than me. I had to be the best and never let myself slow down to rest, mentally or physically.

I would be invited to banquet after banquet, and stand up there giving speeches, accepting all kinds of awards, people patting me on the back. Newspaper articles were calling me a role model. I think my *fatherlessness* was starting to creep in a little bit, just a little bit, because I was at these awards banquets—I was winning this award and that award, and I was a celebrated athlete—and it was just my mom and me. Don't get me wrong, my mom being present was huge. I am so grateful. However, it was always just my mom at the banquets. I would shove those feelings of fatherlessness aside and tell myself I didn't, and was determined not to, need him. After all, not needing him made me feel strong and in control.

> EVERY NOW AND THEN, SUCH AS WHEN I'D SEE OTHER LOVING FATHERS AT THE GAMES... THOSE SUPPRESSED EMOTIONS WOULD START PERCOLATING TO THE SURFACE. MY RESPONSE WOULD BE TO JUST SLAM THE LID BACK DOWN, DIG A LITTLE DEEPER INSIDE, AND FORCE MYSELF TO FOCUS HARDER ON BEING STRONG AND INDEPENDENT.

Outside my mom, however, what I did have was my *band of brothers*—those two best friends, John and Herb. John lived in my neighborhood, and Herb lived not too far from my neighborhood. I considered Herb's family to be well-off. The problem was Herb had convinced himself he would never live past the age of twenty-six because his dad had died suddenly at that age. He lived thinking, "It doesn't matter. I'm not going to live past twenty-six, so what the heck." The absence of his father had dug a deep hole in his soul too, and when we are living out of our pain, we can convince ourselves of all sorts of lies. John, on the other hand, had an absentee father and brothers who were in prison. He spoke often about how Herb and I had become his safe place. Sometimes people would have issues with John's brothers and would want to take it out on him, but knowing we were a band of brothers gave him a safe place. All three of us had men in the house who were not our biological fathers, which brings me back to my mom.

Mom eventually married my youngest brother; Alvin's father and he moved into the house that she had worked so hard to get. What's absurd is on the wedding day they had to go find him and he was at his girlfriend's house. That's how messed up it was. I won't go into all the details, but the verbal and physical abuse was brutal. They used to get into arguments, and I tried to say something one time, but he took me out on the porch and said, "Stay in your place, boy. Just don't mind grown folks' business." As I grew bigger and stronger and the abuse intensified, I finally faced off with him. I threw his stuff outside and kicked him out of the house because the situation had become so toxic. I looked at my mom and said, "If you ever let him come back, you'll never see this face again. You'll never see me again." I was desperate to see her get out of the situation she was in, and I knew it would take something drastic like this to stop the cycle of breaking up, making up, in and out, that was bad and getting worse.

In my band of brothers, we were all great athletes in our own right and well known in Sarasota. We were the cream of the crop and the prospects that everybody believed in. John and Herb played other sports, but primarily when the three of us were together, our focus was on football. "One for all, all for one" was our motto. If I had it, they had it. If they had it, I had it. But as I said before, we were orphans, fatherless boys raising each other. We didn't do the best job because we were all into some of the same things—the girls, the parties, the weekend, the lies, the cheating, the immorality. I started treating women badly in high school. What I did not want for my mom—for her to be in pain, to suffer, to be used by men—is exactly what I became to other girls. I became the very thing I despised.

This is common for orphans. An orphan aches for home yet can never seem to find it, so the quest for that place of belonging, that place that brings inner calm, becomes relentless. Again and again, they become disappointed, unfulfilled, and hurt. The more they come up short, the more desperate their souls become. Orphans can never just relax and exhale in *who* they are and *why* they are, even if their outer facade depicts success and happiness. Someone can even have a wonderful earthly father and family and still be an orphan in spirit, experiencing "comfortlessness" in their souls. Always searching for that place of inner home, even subconsciously, orphans are wounded and feel like outcasts who don't belong, like square pegs in round holes. The sad truth is, Satan has basically turned the world into an orphanage, and we have a culture living out of their pain. All you have to do is watch the news. School shootings, riots, violent mobs, all living out of their pain. Pain doesn't excuse wrong behavior, but it does explain it. If I don't know the truth about who I am and the answer to the questions of where *home* is—whom I belong to, where I fit in—then I'm going to reach for a lot of different things. Some of those things I reach for and attach to may feel better than others, but every one of them eventually loses their ability to bring completeness. None will be the answer to the one thing needed to carry me through the long journey of life and beyond. We were three orphans raising one another while living out of our pain.

And while wrapped in the outward trappings of athletic success, I was inwardly becoming what I hated.

However, there was a love and a bond among our band of brothers that ran deep. While I had a good relationship with my brothers and sister, my identity wasn't shaped by them. I loved them; we loved each other. We had fun growing up. All that was true. But it felt as though Herb and John were my soulmates. We were inseparable. As we grew in athletics, popularity—all those things gave us influence, reasons to be, a place. This was who we were. This was our world.

Finally, it came down to the time when I had to decide on which college I was going to attend, and I was getting offers from everywhere—UCLA, USC, Ohio State, Michigan, Florida State, Florida, Miami, Alabama, LSU, Penn State, you name it. They invited me to visit, and I went to a few. John and Herb were also getting offers from some of the same schools that I was.

One very wealthy alumnus from a school in Florida owned a car dealership and was recruiting me for that school. The two of us were sitting there in his car, and he knew I was going to have to make a decision. He was speaking to me about what he was worth and basically how I could be taken care of if I ended up going to this one particular institution. I understood exactly what he was saying. I would've had a car, a credit card, money in my pocket—never lacking. This was before what's called Name, Image, and Likeness (NIL), through which college athletes can receive compensation. Everything would've been covered, even anything I needed for my mom. It was that level. Yet I was sitting there thinking, "I can't do this." I was aware that some of the players I knew had gone off to college and been taken care of. When they came back, they didn't know how to take care of themselves. I was sitting there questioning it: "It's true that I need every bit of what he's offering because I don't have much. But if he takes care of me, I'll never learn how to take care of myself, and who's going to take care of me when I'm finished?" It was that self-responsibility kicking in, which was a good thing in so many instances.

As I pondered and thought through it, I made the decision. I had to go to the most difficult place to see if I could become a man and actually make it—I had no father, and I couldn't depend on someone else. That was my plan A: Go someplace where all this stuff isn't being offered to me. "I'm going to have to figure it out," I thought. "I'm going to have to work hard. I'm going to have to find out who I am, and if I don't make it, I'm still young enough to bounce back and figure out my plan B."

Dave Truitt was another surrogate whom the Father put in my path at a critical moment in my life. He actually coached at Riverview High School, the rival high school across town. I knew him from when he coached at Ringling Redskins Park when I was a little kid in Pop Warner. What I didn't know was Mr. Truitt had been tracking me through the years. He knew what was going on with me with recruiting and contacted Penn State to recruit me. I finally made a visit to Penn State, the last visit I made. They were preparing for the national championship game against Georgia and Herschel Walker in the Sugar Bowl. Penn State legends including quarterback Todd Blackledge and running back Curt Warner were playing. It was a very big deal. I was up in Pennsylvania during that week and being from Florida didn't have much by way of winter clothes. I remember being out there freezing my butt off, and they hesitated to give me a sweatshirt. Someone had to go see if it was in the rules to allow me to be given a sweatshirt so I wouldn't freeze.

Most of the places I visited put athletes up in a hotel. They had beautiful women escorting you around to different places. At Penn State, one of the most prestigious universities in the nation, I stayed in a dorm with two other football players and slept on a cot. I saw academic advisers and life on the campus, understanding where I would be and the community I would be engaged in. They didn't offer me anything other than a full scholarship and the opportunity to play for one of the top teams in the country that had produced NFL-caliber players. I thought, "This is where I've got to go. This is the place that will prepare me to survive and learn how to become a man."

After that visit, back home before signing day, the pressure got so intense in the recruiting process that I left my house and stayed with Mr. Truitt and his family until it was over. I had been getting a steady stream of nasty messages filled with threats such as, "If you go to Penn State, or anywhere out of state, don't come back to Florida. Why are you doing this? Don't take the talent out of Florida." Even some of the in-state universities were telling me, "If you leave, you'll never get a job in Florida." These alumni groups are pretty powerful people and know how to apply the pressure. Thankfully, Mr. Truitt became a buffer. Finally, I realized it didn't matter what anybody was saying. I knew what I needed to do. "No one's going to help me become a man. No one's going to be able to get me where I think I need to be." I didn't have the clearest picture, but I knew there was something else that I needed to find out: "Who am I actually going to become as a man?"

Two days after Penn State won that national championship, Joe Paterno was sitting in my house with Mr. Truitt, talking to my mom. The next day, he was at my high school. There was a media fest because he could have been at any one of the twenty thousand high schools, but he was at mine. And I thought Coach Paterno was a long-lost grandpapa because I had started with an Italian man, and now this Italian man was coming in my life who was a lot like Coach Patella. Mr. Truitt and his family remained lifelong friends of mine. I did the eulogy at his funeral.

I did sign with Penn State. However, after I signed, I still had to finish my senior year in Florida before reporting for training camp that summer. Before I went, Mr. Truitt made one more key connection for me. He introduced me to an elite trainer, a kinesiologist named Dr. Mattes, who became another critical surrogate in my life. He took me on as his personal project, and I would spend three, four hours a night, five nights a week, at his house working out in his garage. He never charged me a penny, and he and his wife would let me eat dinner with them. He was a beautiful man with a beautiful family. As a result of him taking me in and training me, I became stronger than I had ever been and ran faster than I had ever run. When I reported to play for Joe Paterno, I was in the best shape of my life physically and mentally, which enabled me to play my freshman year.

As for Herb and John, Herb wound up signing with Florida State, and John went to the University of Tampa on a basketball scholarship. He was great at both football and basketball but leaned more toward the latter. We had made a pact that we would all go to the same college, but life didn't work out that way. Leaving Sarasota to go to Pennsylvania was a painful experience. Herb and I were at the airport, and we knew our lives would never be the same again. As we embraced, the reality of the life we had as brothers was changing. Me, I was going off into the unknown, alone.

After I was at Penn State, I found out Coach Paterno was as much a military general as a loving grandpa. A strong disciplinarian, his goal was to make you what he saw, not what you thought you were. He made me mad and dig deeper. He pushed me to the edge, to the point that I wanted to quit Penn State. It was just too much. But Joe Paterno saw something in me I didn't see in myself, and thankfully I didn't quit. He helped me find something more inside me.

And back in high school when I had been thinking, "I need to go to a difficult place. I need to go to a place where I'm going to be forced to learn and figure out who I am, because I didn't know"—that's exactly what happened.

CHAPTER 6

STANDING TO MY FEET

In high school I had been a big man on campus, but now, at Penn State, everybody had been the big dog in their high school. All of us were cream-of-the-crop athletes, and the competition was fierce. There was no lack of testosterone pumping, or egos sizing each other up. We were a team doing life together, but make no mistake about it, we were competitors, and it was intense. For those first few weeks, in July and August, when we had two or three practices a day, it was like Army boot camp. I was homesick and lonely, with a hollow feeling in the pit of my stomach. Of course, the coaches getting in your face, yelling and blowing loud whistles like drill sergeants, only magnified my emotional state. I would get more adjusted to the routines of college life when the rest of the students got back on campus, classes started, and the football season was underway, but when I first arrived for training camp, I can remember walking through that locker room and dorm thinking, "This is home now, and it is going to be tough."

It was a whole different world for me. I'd been up there for my exciting recruiting visit, but after I formally moved there to live, reality started setting in. Everything I had thought I was going to face was here, right now—the challenge of being in a new environment, stepping into a new world, stepping into the unknown. "Can I make it? Is this going to work? How about my academics?" A gazillion questions were going through my head. Oh, and by the way, I had to survive on this football team with the likes of all these huge, gifted, established athletes. That sense of wanting to measure up never left me. This reality kept me urgent and intentional about the conversation I had had with the man in the suit back in junior high. Determination, motivation, discipline, and perseverance—all those things still applied. That imaginary guy who was bigger and faster than me had morphed into actual guys who were bigger and faster than me.

On a lighter note, that helps paint the picture. Once, earlier, I had gotten into a fight on the field. And while I was fighting, Coach Paterno yelled, "Johnson, get out of here! Get out of here!" I didn't know what that meant. I thought he was telling me to leave and not come back, so I just started running to the locker room. When Coach saw me running, he said, "Keep going; keep going. Go back to Flaurida. Go back to Flaurida." When I got in the locker room, I thought, "What am I supposed to do now?" Later my teammates said, "When he does that, go to the sideline." No doubt, Coach Joe Paterno was hard, but through the years, I would come to understand that he was trying to pull that something extra out of me and all of us.

After those first grueling practices in August of my freshman year, fall finally was in the air, much earlier in Pennsylvania than in Florida, and we played our first game of the season, which was also my first collegiate game. I had worked hard in training camp and knew my stuff. We were playing Nebraska in the Kickoff Classic in the Meadowlands, which is Giants Stadium, located in New Jersey, outside of New York City. They were the preseason number one. Penn State had won the national championship the previous year. Even though I thought I was prepared physically, I was still a freshman, and being mentally prepared was something else.

I had played in high school in front of pretty good crowds of around five thousand, but to finally run into a college football stadium and see seventy thousand people in the stands was mesmerizing. On top of that, those Cornhuskers out there looked huge, and it was intimidating to be in this NFL stadium playing against this team that looked like an NFL team. I was actually a little bit afraid, yet not totally afraid, because I never figured I would play as a freshman. In those days it was unusual for freshmen to even travel, let alone see any playing time. I was fortunate to get to travel and experience the game, but I had no expectations of actually getting into the game. I would soon have a wake-up call.

Around the second or third series in the game Coach Paterno started calling out my name. "Johnson! Johnson!" I thought, "He can't be calling me; he can't be calling me right now." But he was. "Get in there! Get in there!" The guy who played ahead of me had lost his shoe. I didn't want to go in, but obviously I had to. Now, I knew my stuff inside and out because at Penn State, you've got to be sharp. You have to know your assignment. You have to work hard, rehearse, and be on point. I had done all that, yet when I got in the game, my mind went blank. I mean, I didn't remember a thing. Maybe I got in a huddle, but they called whatever defense, and I was standing out there on the left side as a defensive end. It was all a blur because I didn't remember the defense, I didn't know what I was supposed to do, and I was looking at all these guys on the offensive line who looked as though they had meat hooks coming from their arms. They were massive. The ball was hiked, and I just reacted and went forward, and nobody blocked me. I couldn't believe it! I had a wide-open shot into the backfield, and they handed the ball off to Mike Rozier, who, by the way, won the Heisman Trophy. I was one-on-one with him. Now, this was becoming a dream come true, my chance to be a hero. I was in the backfield. I tried to go get him. He made a move. He juked, I hit his feet, and he sped up. He just kept going, leaving me in the dust. I felt so dumb because not only did I know what to do, but I had a perfect setup to make a big play in the backfield. Instead, I don't think I even slowed the guy down. That's a picture of how I was in over my head where I was.

Somehow I made it through my first season. It wasn't great, but I survived. Then, a few months later, after spring practices, going into my sophomore year, I had to have knee surgery. Fortunately, rehab was quick, and I was able to play that season. However, I was in a very difficult place. The pressure was mounting, and I felt I was in over my head. I just wasn't handling things mentally as well. So they sent me to the psychologist. They were trying to figure me out; I was trying to figure me out. I don't know how long it was. There were times when I sat in my room and was trying to figure out how to get home. I wanted to leave. I remember one spring when I was sitting at a window—it was April 27, and there was twenty-seven inches of snow on the ground. I thought, "What am I doing? I gotta get out." But I had no money.

I had had a lot of struggles along the way. For several counseling sessions we talked about my life and whatever I was going through. He gave me some guidance, but it didn't really seem to make a difference, because it wasn't the answer I needed. Yet I refused to tuck my tail between my legs and go home. Instead of quitting, I just kept pressing forward, working it out, muscling through, trying to figure things out myself.

It was complicated because I knew it was going to be hard. I just didn't know it was going to be *that* hard to manage school, football, and life. Penn State didn't give you grades. They gave you academic advisers who helped you work and assigned you to study hall. You had to earn everything. I had to learn to manage my time. Classes were at a certain time, workouts a certain time, team meetings, practices. And being late wasn't an option. Coach Paterno showed little tolerance for tardiness. If there was a team meeting at a certain time and you were even a couple of minutes late, you had to run before or after practice. It's common for college players to have recurring nightmares that they are late to meetings or practices! On top of that, my vehicle was my two legs. I had to walk across campus or catch a ride with one of my teammates. Instead of going home for the summer, I worked at Woodward Camp those months just to get a bicycle. It was a really nice Schwinn road bike. The camp was located outside Penn State and was where many of the Olympic athletes would train.

What I didn't know was the Father had been working through all this as He'd always been working, preparing me my whole life. Back during my freshman year, He divinely set me up with D.J. Dozier as my roommate. D.J. was an incredible athlete who would have careers in the NFL as a running back with the Minnesota Vikings and Detroit Lions and in MLB as an outfielder for the New York Mets. That is rare. Not only would D.J. and I become lifelong friends but God would use him in my life there at Penn State, and then to speak prophetically into my life decades later, as you will see. In the beginning, however, neither D.J. nor I was serving the Lord. During orientation his parents went to a church service while visiting, but we did not go. That didn't matter; his mother still arranged for the pastor to follow up with D.J. And he was faithful to do just that, which would include me. The problem was D.J. and I were both running as far away as we could from anything with the likes of religion or Jesus. We wanted to live our lives and do what we wanted to do. Parties, chasing girls—we wanted to do all that. Let your imagination run with that a bit to catch who we were. We did that. And we did it well. Wherever we went, we went together. During freshman year, he was a sinner, and so was I. He was a "religious sinner" because he grew up in church. I was just a sinner. That pastor whom D.J.'s mom asked to follow up pursued him every chance he got—but D.J. used to hide from the guy. He ran from him and avoided his phone calls all the time. And I would lie for him every time he needed me to.

I remember going to one Bible study and never going back because some of the same guys who were there saying they were Christian were also at the parties, drinking and womanizing, doing the same things I was doing. I wasn't a Christian and never claimed to be. I didn't know the *real* Jesus yet, but I did know I despised hypocrites. So quietly, I just never went back and resolved in my mind that I didn't know God, but if I ever did know Him, it wouldn't look like that. Still, the pastor who followed up with us had faithfully planted a seed. That seed would begin to germinate.

That year, as a sophomore, was brutal. Not only was I coming off surgery and rehab, but after the season I ended up back in the hospital with what they thought was minor spinal meningitis, which is deadly. They did a spinal tap in my back with a needle about the size of a sixteen-penny nail, with no anesthesia. I had never felt a pain like that. The only pain I can imagine coming close is labor pains. I was in the hospital for about a week, laid out on my back, wondering what was going to happen to me. No one had answers. I was all alone. D.J. and a couple of teammates visited me, but Mom was not there to tenderly care. No one could help me. I had no father to call or show up. Lying in that hospital bed, I began to cry out to God. I was saying, "God, if You're there, if You help me, I'll read my Bible." I had never prayed sincerely like that before, and I was thinking this was a compelling negotiation I was making. I don't even know if I called it a prayer. It was more a cry of desperation because I was at my end. All I had invested in was my physical ability to go further, to test myself, to find out what was in me and what I was made of. And I had hit a wall. Now I was on my back, looking up. How appropriate.

THE PASTOR WHO FOLLOWED UP WITH US HAD FAITHFULLY PLANTED A SEED. THAT SEED WOULD BEGIN TO GERMINATE.

After I got out of the hospital, I tried to read my Bible for a couple of weeks, then put it down because it was incomprehensible to me, every part of it. So I did away with that and went back to how I had been living.

Coming out of the hospital, I went right into winter conditioning, and there was an incident. Because it gets so cold in the winters up there, we were training in the Bubble, which is our indoor practice facility. We were running shuttle runs, like gassers, which is basically sprinting from sideline to sideline twice. You had to make them within a certain time, or the whole group had to do it over. I had lost weight, fifteen to twenty pounds, and was still weak. I was doing OK, but toward the end I became overly exhausted. But again, I purposed to muscle through—but this time I couldn't. Coach Paterno was watching, and he called me out. I mean, he chewed me out, and my teammates picked me up and dragged me across the finish line. I ended up having to go into the training room after that just to recover. No one had told Coach that I'd been in the hospital. He came in and apologized. I'm no slouch. I'm not a person who's going to cut corners, and it did a lot for me to see a man of his stature do what he did, because I revered him. I respected Joe Paterno. The fact that he drilled me to the ground and was grinding me but then came back and apologized really helped me understand something. When you have authority, it defines, shapes, and builds up. Yet it can also be used in humility. There's not much more powerful and affirming than a person who has authority having enough security to humble themself and admit they made a mistake.

After that incident of having my teammates drag me to the finish line, I got stronger and back into the kind of condition that I needed to be in for the spring practices. Coach Paterno was calling me into who I was going to be. While I was simply looking at where I was right then, he always saw something greater, deeper, those nuggets, and was trying to mine them to the surface. He succeeded, because I was named co-MVP for the spring game.

After that spring, there was a big campus outreach taking place with former Penn State quarterback Todd Blackledge, who'd been a first-round draft pick in the NFL and was playing for the Kansas City Chiefs. There were a couple of other former Penn State players who were now in the NFL. We would gawk at them because they were where we dreamed of being. We were fan boys. Whatever they were doing, whatever they wanted to say, we were there. They ended up having a meeting at a church, the First Assembly of State College. Obviously, I was going to go because I wanted to hear what these guys had to say, particularly Todd Blackledge. I went to the church, and this particular event was just for the Penn State football players, so not a whole lot of guys were there.

Todd was standing up there reading the Bible and preaching, and I was amazed because he would say it as if he knew what the Bible said, quoting scriptures. I was sitting there thinking, "I've never seen anything like this." I'm just now revealing this, but my family's spiritual history is Jehovah's Witness, which I came to realize is a false religion. When I was a preteen, we would go to the Kingdom Hall, and I would sit there, clueless as to what they were saying. I would count the letters on the wall behind the preacher, and it was so disconnected from me.

But Todd was preaching, and something inside me was moved by his words. They were alive. It was real. "You're supposed to live like this," I thought. I was gripped. Then, at the end he said, "Does anybody have any questions?" I had a bunch, and he patiently answered them. Other people had questions too.

After the Q and A, Todd said, "Does anybody want to make a stand for Jesus?" I was all in until he said that. I went from the edge of my seat to the back of my seat quickly because of all the guys present and knowing what they really were, hypocrites. I started to notice them. When it was time to stand, I looked around and got afraid. I hesitated and thought, "I can't be saying these guys are hypocrites because I know me. I know what I do. I know what I like to do. I don't know how this is ever going to work." Despite the war going on in my mind, out of nowhere I found myself standing on my feet. Then a couple of my teammates stood up as well. We walked forward and prayed the prayer of salvation with Todd.

I didn't feel much. No goose bumps, no warm sensation flowing through me, nothing. Yet deep down in my gut I knew this was my life, that I was supposed to live like this. I wish I could say everything changed in that moment, but it didn't. The event left town. There was nobody to disciple me. I didn't even know what discipleship was. I still had those sinful desires and went back into my life of sin.

Something had happened inside me, though. There had been a shift in my thinking and my heart. D.J. and I would sit up in our room and have in-depth conversations about God and about Jesus. We had never really done that before. He knew way more than I did. All I knew was I was hungry and wanted to know the truth.

As I was pursuing the truth, a couple of things happened. First, I went back home for a visit, and while I was there, one of the Jehovah's Witnesses came to the house to do a study with us. At that time, I wasn't too aware of their false doctrine, and for some reason, their words didn't connect. When I got back to school, I did a study of the *New World Translation* and the Holy Bible. While researching, I happened upon John chapter 1, and that became the focus of my study. "In the beginning was the Word, and the Word was with God, and the Word was God" (John 1:1). It became crystal clear to me that Jesus *is* God. Looking back, I now know it was the Holy Spirit inside me guiding me to that verse—with my limited biblical knowledge, I probably never would have found it on my own. In the *New World Translation* that verse says, "In the beginning was the Word, and the Word was with God, and the Word was a god." Not "*was God.*" That's a big difference that changes everything.

So when I had another break, I went home and invited the Jehovah's Witnesses back over because I knew Jesus is real. He saved my life. I wanted my family to know, but this false doctrine is all they knew. When they came over, I had my notes and questions. I was ready. I invited him in, and before we get started, I asked some questions. Mainly, I asked about the John 1:1 contrast between the *New World Translation* and the Holy Bible. As I asked, they twisted my words without giving a straight answer. Then, instead of engaging in honest dialogue, they began to antagonize me. "Oh, you done become a preacher," they mocked. "Look at you now." Instead of being patient and loving, I got so frustrated and ended up in an argument that didn't go well, without any of my questions being answered. I ended up on my knees, crying to my mom, my brother, and my sister, saying, "Y'all got to know, Jesus is real. You have to believe me. You have to believe me." But I looked wrong, as if I didn't have a handle on things, because when they suckered me in, I was arguing with them.

When I returned to Penn State after that break, however, it was just like the Father to bring into D.J.'s and my lives some godly men who really had a heart for us and just loved on us, poured into us, taught us the Bible, and began to disciple us. They were elders and leaders from Unity Christian Fellowship, an on-fire church with a campus outreach. Not unity as in Unitarian, but a solid Bible-believing church. These men moved in the power and love of the Holy Spirit. It changed my life because D.J. and I learned the importance of prayer, and how to pray in the Holy Spirit, study the Word, and live a life of giving. Unity rescued me out of spiritual mediocrity because I was floundering. Between the elders, the pastor, and D.J.'s youth pastor, who came and prayed over us and really encouraged us, I started to get rooted. I started to get grounded. I started to grab hold of what life in Jesus was about. It was awesome. I had never really gone to church like that, where I was growing in my relationship with Jesus. It was everything I needed. It started in the spring of my senior year, during the offseason. D.J. and I would have Friday night prayer. I was involved in the young leaders training—there was a group of young leaders that the senior pastor would disciple and train in leadership. It was when D.J.'s youth pastor came up and prayed for us that I received the gift of tongues. My life changed in such a profound way it was unbelievable. Jesus became real to me. I even prayed for people and saw them healed. D.J.'s life started changing profoundly too. We would grow together. We started a Bible study in our dorm, shared our faith, and prayed for students and teammates.

Once, one of our teammates who was into partying and cheating on his girlfriend came busting in our dorm room, white as a sheet. He was really scared. He said, "Y'all have got to pray for me. Do you know what just happened to me?" He explained that while he was in bed, he was suddenly pinned down by an evil force. He couldn't move, couldn't speak. All he could do was think about Jesus, and when he said the name Jesus, it left. We prayed over their beds, their shoes, their pillows. Some guys got mad at us because we were having Bible studies and they wanted to have parties. That was part of the contention.

One example of how my heart was changing was when I happened upon a hundred dollars. You would have thought that I, being a broke college student, won the lottery. Then, the Holy Spirit nudged me and said, "Give it all away this Sunday." And I thought, "That ain't God. That's got to be the devil. Ain't no way in the world." And I remember sitting in church, thinking, "I can't. I got to eat." I didn't have much of anything outside of whatever they fed us in the cafeteria and the training table. "So I'm preserving this hundred dollars I got," I thought. By the end of the service, it was as though it was burning in my hand. I went up to the pastor and just offered it. And I believe the Holy Spirit said, "I wanted to test you to see if what I give you, you will give back to Me because there's so much more." There was so much more He wanted to do and to give me. That little bit of money was just a test.

On the football side, things really accelerated. My junior year we were undefeated and played against Oklahoma for the national championship in the Orange Bowl in Miami. We lost. That winter Coach Paterno got the whole team together when most teams were taking a break and doing whatever. He called a team meeting and said, "I want you to remember what you felt to lose. I want you to remember how that felt after the game." And he said, "I want everybody to do at least one thing every day until the season starts, to be a champion, to put yourself in the position to have that opportunity again."

He was telling us to go to class, be on time. Do our work. Do our workout, conditioning. Do one thing. He was saying to mentally put ourselves in a position where we were doing at least one thing a day that would prepare us to be champions. I think everybody did it because we were playing that game all year before we had to play our next season. We went through my senior season undefeated again and made it back to the national championship game. At the time, the most popular show on television was *Miami Vice*, and they moved it and put our game in its time slot because this was the most-watched college football game in the history of college football up to that point.

That year, I got my degree in four years when other players were fine with five years or longer. Graduating in four years is kind of a big deal for collegiate football players because of all the pressure and distractions of practice and games and traveling. Even so, I took a full load of classes every semester. In the fall of my senior year, during football season, I loaded the deck with eighteen credits. I said to myself, "I must have a degree when I leave here, because so often guys leaving don't come back. And that's an incomplete in their lives. So I have to take care of this responsibility. No one is going to make sure I do it but me."

During one of the games of my senior season, I had so much work to do. I had my book bag in the back of the bus. We rode school buses over from our training facility to the stadium because it was a little too far to walk. We drove the bus there, and I got my book bag, put it in my locker, and went out and played four quarters in front of a capacity crowd of more than eighty-three thousand. We won. Back in the locker room I took off my uniform, showered, iced, and got dressed. But instead of celebrating with the guys and getting caught up in all the activities, I got my backpack and walked through all the tailgate parties straight to the library. It was probably about two miles or so after a long, hot day out. Beaver Stadium was kind of off campus out there. I was exhausted, of course, and went up to the top floor of the library. I laid my head down and took a nap because I knew I would be no good if I didn't sleep for at least a little bit. I just stayed there to get my work done. I wasn't putting all my eggs in the basket of "I'm going to make it to the NFL." I didn't want to be that guy. I didn't want to be stereotyped by anybody. I didn't want to come out of college thinking about just athletics, sports, and the NFL, with no college degree. Sure, I wanted to play in the NFL, but did I absolutely need to? Not really. That was my mindset. The only person that was going to take care of me was me. All that focus and extreme work ethic were wonderful and contributed to my success. Mom taught me well. Yet it was also a way to suppress what was going on deep inside me. I became a master at keeping those inner gnawings at bay.

I was now saved by the blood of Jesus, yet I was still struggling with a sinful lifestyle and those inner feelings of orphanhood. The good news was the Father was still working, bringing me to the next place. I was very new in my faith and was willing to do whatever the Lord wanted me to do.

There was a difference between my will and the Father's will. I had reached my capacity. I had reached the limits of my ability. I was maxing out, had no regrets, no hesitation. I was moving forward at full speed. This shift spiritually was sort of the same. There was no difference that became extremely noticeable in my first year or so of figuring this out. I didn't know what I was doing. My life looked as though I was a sinner. I still had the desires of my flesh mixed with the reality that I couldn't shake. I knew I was supposed to live differently. All the times I had known there was something uncommon that I was supposed to pursue and do, I did it. I had this sense in a spiritual way, but I couldn't do it. I didn't know how to do it. I had to be convinced myself in order for it to change my life. No one was ever going to take away that little bitty kernel of truth I had. That set a different precedent and pace for my openness not to just any old thing but to who Jesus is. I could really begin to go down the road when we got connected back in my junior year to Unity Christian Fellowship. That made all the difference in the world. This small church was part of my life change because I began to get taught the Bible in a more formal setting.

CHAPTER 7

ENCOUNTER WITH LOVE

had stood to my feet in front of my teammates at the Todd Blackledge outreach, unashamedly walked up front, put my trust in Jesus to save my life. I had asked some questions and had gotten some answers. Mainly, I was growing into the understanding of who Jesus is. He is God. Although it was a rather unemotional moment and I left that night not feeling much different from before, something real had happened. An authentic transaction had taken place that the Father would honor. Having said that, I walked out of that meeting right back into my lifestyle of sin. Truth be told, I was still running and still had so many more questions with no real discipleship. Though I'd found salvation, I didn't understand my true identity and sank right back into my old, fleshly nature because that was the most comfortable thing for me to do. I remember telling D.J. that I had been messing around with this lady and doing things I shouldn't. I said, "D.J., I like sin. I like sin. I like it." Yet I knew I wasn't supposed to live in it. A part of me was actively pursuing God, longing for Him. I was just fumbling and stumbling along, struggling with how to walk it out. This was a whole new world. When you don't know whom you belong to, what your identity is, you don't know how to behave. We'll get more into that later in the book. But now, what was noticeably new for me was I couldn't stay comfortable in my sin. Unlike before, an uneasiness now came along with it: conviction. The Holy

Spirit had moved inside me, even though I didn't know what was going on. And when the Holy Spirit moves in, He brings in new furniture and destroys the old. That's what He does. A shift was taking place in my spirit man.

It's important to note here how the Father, in His grace, creates space for us to grow into who we are. There are a lot of people who enter churches, give their lives to the Lord, and are sometimes delivered instantly from things. Other times—most of the time—it's a process to get used to the new furniture. I was in process. And the Father's grace was on me.

A PART OF ME WAS ACTIVELY PURSUING GOD, LONGING FOR HIM. I WAS JUST FUMBLING AND STUMBLING ALONG, STRUGGLING WITH HOW TO WALK IT OUT.... BUT NOW, WHAT WAS NOTICEABLY NEW FOR ME WAS I COULDN'T STAY COMFORTABLE IN MY SIN.

A good while before the men from Unity Christian Fellowship began discipling us, someone had given me a book by Og Mandino called *The Greatest Salesman in the World*. There was a prayer in the back, and I memorized every single word. I wasn't in church, and no one was really teaching me the Bible. I was struggling with sin, though I knew I was supposed to live differently. I just didn't know how and would say that prayer going to and from class. This was my junior year, and behind our apartments, down by the football complex, was a chicken coop that emitted the strongest stench of chicken poop you ever smelled in your life! I remember passing the chicken coop and saying that prayer I had memorized, called "The Salesman's Prayer," because I was desperate, desperate to see a change. I was not a salesman, just a newly saved college student athlete, but I knew I was supposed to pray. I didn't even know if the prayer was theologically correct.

Nonetheless, I prayed it, and God used it. It's interesting that the mystery man in the suit back in junior high had been a salesman. Here's the prayer I had memorized.

Oh creator of all things, help me. For this day I go out into the world naked and alone, and without your hand to guide me I will wander far from the path which leads me to success and happiness.

I ask not for gold or garments or even opportunities equal to my ability; instead, guide me so that I may acquire ability equal to my opportunities.

You have taught the lion and the eagle how to hunt and prosper with teeth and claw. Teach me how to hunt with words and prosper with love so that I may be a lion among men and an eagle in the market place.

Help me to remain humble through obstacles and failures; yet hide not from mine eyes the prize that will come with victory.

Assign me task to which others have failed; yet guide me to pluck the seeds of success from their failures. Confront me with fears that will temper my spirit; yet endow me with courage to laugh at my misgivings.

Spare me sufficient days to reach my goals; yet help me live this day as if it were my last. Bathe me in good habits that the bad ones may drown; yet grant me compassion for the weaknesses in others. Suffer me to know that all things shall pass; yet help me to count my blessings of today.

Expose me to hate so it be not a stranger; yet fill my cup with love to turn strangers into friends. But all these things be only if thy will. I am a small and lonely grape clutching the vine yet thou hast made me different from all others.

> *Verily, there must be a special place for me. Guide
> me. Help me. Show me the way Lord. Let me become
> all you planned for me when my seed was planted
> and selected by you to sprout in the vineyard of the
> world.*
> *Help this humble salesman.... Guide me, God.*[1]

After some months of struggling trying to understand my identity, and running from it at the same time, I got a chance to meet Leo Wisniewski, whose younger brother played on the team. Leo had played at Penn State too and was in the NFL with the Indianapolis Colts. He and I made a real connection because he was also a defensive lineman, and Leo was open and available to spend extra time with me and talk to me in depth about Jesus.

Leo was gracious enough to invite me to his apartment because he saw how eager I was to learn about Jesus. I jumped at the invitation, which reflected my hunger for more of the Lord and also my wanting to just be closer to Leo. His presence was like a magnet, and he was what I was striving to be like. At the apartment we were talking when suddenly, out of nowhere, this presence descended over me. It felt as if buckets of liquid love, pure and unconditional, were pouring over me like warm, soothing oil, penetrating every crevice of my wounded soul. Time seemed suspended as I was being overwhelmed by an awareness of His presence. Jesus was wrapping His arms around me, embracing me. It was the most profound, tangible, spiritual experience of my life. Supernatural can be evil and dark, or it can be good and light. That is real about this world. I've seen dark before, and it's real. But I had never seen light like this. I was sitting on the floor around a small table, and all of a sudden, I felt as if there was an outpouring of fresh oil. There was a presence. I was being captivated, completely immersed in this feeling of love. It was the most life-changing, deepest experience. It was pure love. That's all I knew. I just felt love as I'd never felt love before.

What's difficult to relate is it wasn't merely a sensation of love, but the love itself was alive, a person. I wasn't in deep prayer or worship or crying out to God or anything like that. I was just sitting there, and *BAM!* He showed up. This was not something I could have prayed for because I wasn't aware something like this could even happen.

Not sure what was going on, instead of trying to figure it out, I just dropped my head and let the Father's waterfall of affection drench me. My surroundings all faded away. I didn't want to move, didn't want to speak, didn't want to do anything but soak up whatever this was. I could have lived right there, forever. If fifty years passed and I was still sitting at the table, that would've been fine with me. I didn't want it to ever stop. In that moment, every desire, thought, idea, plan, pain, and hope disappeared. Everything in my body was completely satisfied as His overwhelming peace melted me. I had no needs, no desires but for whatever was happening to not stop. And it was the love, the presence of love like I did not know existed. My mind was absolutely clear, and all I desired was more of Him. Weeping, I was saying, "Don't leave. Please don't leave. Don't go. Please."

After a while, His presence lifted. Though I couldn't wrap my mind around everything in that moment, I instinctively understood the concentration of that liquid love was Jesus.

Not only was I completely satisfied in His presence, but it also re-created in me a desire to live for that, to live for Him. Everything that I'd been looking for found me. At that point, I still hadn't had any thought or teaching on the Father. Jesus was everything. So it was the love of Jesus that took away every desire in my being except for Him. That encounter was an invitation to pursue His love for the rest of my life. Somehow I knew He would always be with me and that I would never be the same. His presence, that liquid love, was Jesus showing me, telling me, "You belong to Me." It wasn't about my behavior. As time passed and I reflected, the Father showed me that He had graciously given me the encounter because He wanted me to know on the front end of my journey what the rest of the journey was going to be about—Him loving me, and me learning to receive and walk in that love.

In that moment, Jesus became real to me. Before, I had mentally understood that Jesus was God, but now I knew it personally. It wasn't just a seed in my heart saying, "I know I'm supposed to live like this." I had had that already. I just didn't know how. So when that encounter happened, I knew it was undeniable, and it was the love of Jesus.

It changed my life in that I now knew Jesus is real, but surprisingly I still didn't have the way to freedom when my fleshly desires, going to fraternity parties and cheating on my girlfriend and lying about it, came back. And they *did* come back. When His presence was there, nothing else was there. But when His presence lifted, I was back to some of the same fights in my soul, in my mind. I was intent on figuring it out, how to live in the awareness of His presence when I didn't feel it. I was gripped. I felt like the apostle Paul in Romans 7: "For I do not do the good I want to do, but the evil I do not want to do.... But I see another law at work in me.... Thanks be to God, who delivers me through Jesus Christ our Lord!" (vv. 19, 23, 25).

When I had the revelation of who Jesus is and said yes and repented, He revealed to me that I belong to Him. Now He was going to show me how to live in His love. That's the key to this new life, living in His love. I'm surrendering and yielding my heart and mind to learn and to grow in relationship with Him, because now knowing Him is the most important thing. After all, everything we need in life comes out of intimacy with Him.

That said, I still wasn't looking for a father, because I had learned so well not to need one. I didn't want to need something that I had pushed so far underneath the surface of my being. Somewhere in my head I reasoned there were enough surrogates and coaches, along with my uncles, around to buffer what I had already suppressed. I had suppressed the need to where now I didn't want that. When I was younger, I was longing, looking around, but it was short-lived because I didn't have it. And I was actually functioning based on sports and performance and all that activity. I had replaced that hole in my soul with everything I was doing. I didn't need a father, whom I didn't even have an image of. There was no picture.

But the Father was still working. The deeper revelations of my fatherlessness would be revealed over time. He would give me another encounter for that later, in His perfect timing, but now I was being set free by the truth that God loves me, and Jesus was giving me an introduction of what to pursue. "Pursue this love," He whispered to me, "not the lust that you had once called love, not the counterfeit affections you attach yourself to." It was the foundation of being able to walk out of the pain of my past and the disappointment of what I didn't get.

From that moment on, new desires to do things right captivated my heart. I wasn't making this shift in my focus happen. It was the Holy Spirit inside me, Jesus inside me, the Father inside me compelling me. The old was passing away, slowly but surely. I was being loved by the fullness of God in my mess, in my shame, in my pain and rejection. The truth came to me, not just in what I heard but in being loved by Truth Himself. I was loved, even when there was so much unlovable about me.

You know, you can hear about the love of God but hardly believe it because it comes through the filter of the broken love you've seen and the disappointment you've experienced in the past. We don't really have a true framework. I guess the best way to say it is I was baptized by His love. My life changed that day at the table. I have not been perfect in knowing how to love and live in that love. I can tell you that I have not stopped walking toward, and in, that love more. That was about three and a half decades ago. I've been growing in that love more and more. I think that was the stage that was being set for me to forgive my father. In that moment of breakdown I was able to forgive because I was introduced to the love of the Father, through the love of Jesus. When you understand the love of God, every other love that's lesser is the love you no longer want to pursue. For me, love was all about what I could get. I began to understand from that moment that love is what I can give; I don't want to love people based on what I can get.

That experience with the love of God was the foundation of being able to walk out of the pain of my past—the disappointment of what I didn't get. Sometimes the most difficult things in life are not what happened to you but what didn't happen to you. I'd never had that affection, touch, or intimacy with an earthly father. That can be difficult because it's unfamiliar territory. It's not been defined. I've not been defined by my earthly father and told who I am supposed to be. So I had to make it up. When that kind of love is missing from an earthly father, we look for it in other places. It gets perverted. It gets misinterpreted. It gets abused. We end up broken. We know that there is no way to be healed. I believe when the love of God was released upon me and manifested the way it did, that was not just a moment. I had everything I needed—all the security, all the embrace, all the intimacy. He knew me. He understood me, met me, came to get me where I was, allowed me to want nothing less than this kind of love to define my life.

"Pursue this love."

CHAPTER 8

LOVE CHANGES EVERYTHING

Jesus had wrapped His arms around me that day. The Holy Spirit flooded my being and was now most definitely showing me how to get used to the new furniture inside me. Even more so, He was showing me how to walk this new life out. I was wrecked. My old life was wrecked. I didn't know it was possible to live like this, didn't know I could be this free. Young and raw, I had little biblical knowledge, yet the Father, through Jesus, and the Holy Spirit was giving me what I needed in that season. "Pursue *this* love," He told me. Not just any kind of love. Not lust or amorous love but "*this* love," the love that had encountered me. *This* love was a Person, a Person who wanted to flow into me and then out of me into everything I touched. When you are walking in *this* love, it changes everything. God's not trying to change your behavior. He's trying to change your heart. When your heart is changed through love, your behavior follows. Love changes everything and expresses itself through the practical choices we make. And God's love always involves other people, loving people. "Love the Lord your God with all your heart and with all your soul," Jesus said, and, "'Love your neighbor as yourself.' There is no commandment greater than these" (Mark 12:30–31). It's all about love. If you love God with all your heart and love other people, everything else will fall in line. With the new directive to pursue *this* love, I knew to whom I belonged, so I was learning what to believe and how to behave.

At the same time, while I was being wrecked in a wonderful way by this new revelation of love, my senior year at Penn State was a whirlwind of pressure and activity. We'd won the national championship, and I had made the Walter Camp All America Team. The NFL draft was coming up in the spring, and it was exciting to hear my name being tossed around. Would I be picked? Would I be ready? Plus, I was pushing to graduate in four years. A lot was happening, and now there's this holy war raging inside me. I was still struggling with my flesh, being pulled and yanked, trying to live with one foot in the world and one foot in this new kingdom life that I was learning about. Later on I would come to understand that the struggle is good. It's a sign that something is going on inside you. Those who don't struggle with sin likely don't have the Holy Spirit in them. Up until the table encounter with love, I had been a womanizer and cheater. Oh, I had a big smile that could charm the best of them, but my sinful desires ruled me.

IF YOU LOVE GOD WITH ALL YOUR HEART AND LOVE OTHER PEOPLE, EVERYTHING ELSE WILL FALL IN LINE.

As I mentioned, through high school I had become just like the men I disdained. Though I never was a physical abuser, I was a user. Cheating was the norm when it came to women. This is not a pretty picture, but it's reality. My mom and sister were somehow different, and I protected them from men like me. I did not want them to be in pain, to suffer, to be used by men. I didn't want them to be lied to or cheated on. Yet what I did not want for them, I had become to other girls. During high school, I met Le'Chelle, my wife-to-be, who is more than I deserved. She was, and is, the love of my life, yet I still cheated on her in high school and college. I was in love with her but didn't know how to love her. When we first started dating, I actually had a girlfriend and was trying to secretly juggle both, which is a recipe for disaster. I got found out.

One day a girl I knew as a friend because she was a cheerleader for the football team knocked on the door to my classroom and asked, "Can I see Tim Johnson?" I was thinking, "Why does she want to see me? Why is she pulling me out of class?" Then, when I stepped out of class to see what she wanted, my girlfriend was standing behind her where I couldn't see her until I got out of the classroom, a complete setup. All of a sudden, I realized I was in trouble, and she came after me, chasing me with her purse, so I ran through the math department with her chasing me, steaming mad because I didn't tell her I had another girlfriend. I should've taken my clues not to mess up before this happened because another time, before she found out I'd been secretly seeing Le'Chelle, she looked at me while wielding a knife and said, "If you ever leave me, I'll kill you." In full transparency that scared me a little bit but not enough to get free from living in my sinful desires. After running through the math department, I realized I needed to break up with her and just focus on being with Le'Chelle, who by this time I was sure would be happy to have me all to herself. Breaking up with my girlfriend was not about what she threatened to do to me as much as it was about how badly I treated her, then made it look as if she was the bad person when it was I. Once I broke up with her, I couldn't wait to call Le'Chelle and give her the good news about breaking up. When I called Le'Chelle and said, "Hey, I broke up with her," and she replied, "So?" I was completely caught off guard. "So?" I didn't see that coming. I was all jammed up with nothing to say, and I don't know how the conversation ended because I was not prepared for that response. When she found out I was seeing her and my girlfriend, she wanted nothing to do with me. I was in for a long journey to be with this woman I loved but didn't know how to love yet.

When I went off to Penn State, Le'Chelle went to Florida State. Somehow we maintained our connection through the separation. The spark remained. After I had stood up and said, "Yes," to Jesus that day with Todd Blackledge, and after the encounter with love at the table, Le'Chelle came to visit during a big game weekend. We wound up spending the night together. She went back to Florida State, and we stayed in touch. We loved each other, but neither of us knew how to live for the Father. So, for the five years I had known her and dated her, I had cheated and lied to her. Then, I was genuinely saved yet still living in sin.

Not long after my encounter with pure love at the table and the Lord showing me what to pursue, we found out Le'Chelle was pregnant. It couldn't have come at a more inconvenient time. After all, the national championship game was coming up. I was graduating and possibly embarking on a new career in the NFL. You can imagine how difficult that conversation was, finding out we were pregnant. Some of it is a blur because so much was at stake. I had to be focused on the game, try to finish my degree, try to live right, all those things. Now, "Wait, what? What am I going to do?" I heard different voices. Some suggested having an abortion. After our initial conversation, part of me was numb. I couldn't believe this was happening. Then part of me had no idea what to do. I was going to familiar voices that had been in my life, so part of me wanted to listen to those. It was an easy way out to just get an abortion. But I knew that was not what I wanted to do. I didn't know how to handle this situation. There was no father around to talk to about it. My identity was at stake; everything was in front of me. I was at a crossroads again, trying to figure out life decisions that were going to alter everything.

I knew the national championship was coming. We would be on the world's stage. It was a lot to deal with emotionally. Practice didn't let up. The heat in Arizona didn't let up. The media fest was crazy. That national championship week was the wildest thing. The tension between us and Miami had us ready to get it on in a parking lot. Case in point: We went to a big cookout with both teams, where a talent show was lined up between the teams. It was supposed to be a festive, fun thing. They were up first, and Jerome Brown got up and said, "Did the Japanese eat with the Americans before they bombed Pearl Harbor? No." And they walked off and left the event. I was on fire. We all were on fire. We wanted to get it on right then, go to the parking lot and play the game there with no pads. If you would have lit a match, the whole place would have blown up, there was so much heat in the room. So I had that world I was in every day in practice. Then they moved the game to an earlier time, which I think was the first time the NCAA had ever done that. *Miami Vice*, a top show at that time, was moved to a different time just to present this national championship game. It was the most-watched game in college football history at that time.

All that week were events surrounding the national championship. Then I went to a Fellowship of Christian Athletes (FCA) banquet. I still remember one of the most powerful messages I heard from Joe Paterno. He talked about Jesus and how He is the toughest person who ever lived. He talked about what Jesus did that none of us would or could do. He talked about the punishment of His cross, the pain, and all that He did. Hearing about Jesus being tough was quite different from the stained-glass-window Jesus with the sheep around his neck. Joe presented a different picture that I grabbed hold of in my heart. So there was a lot going on. Then I had my pregnant girlfriend on my mind. I didn't even know what to do.

Le'Chelle was still in school, soon to be graduating, with dreams and a bright future. People close to me were telling me that I should probably have the baby aborted. My flesh wanted to agree with them, but the Holy Spirit, who was now inside me, clearly said, "No. The baby is a person that I love....I want you to man up and marry Le'Chelle." That was a strong order, but the Holy Spirit wasn't done. "You've got to tell her the truth about everything, all the women you've been with." Now, being propelled by *this* love, before I marry this girl, *if* she will even have me, she has to know the truth about who I am. Like a floodlight shining into a dark alley, the truth of who I'd been was about to be exposed. At the same time, however, there was a grace present with me that my old man was dead and my new man was emerging. The Father was calling me out based on what He saw me becoming, just as Coach Joe Paterno had done my freshman year based on what he saw me becoming, not my performance. Pursuing *this* life of love was becoming practical and real. How would I respond?

With no real father to talk to, I was trying to figure out how to be a man. I was just listening to the voices that were familiar, until I really knew I heard the voice of truth. Because I lived a lie a long time. And I knew that was familiar; I knew what that was like because I had been living that way. Now I had a decision to make about how my life should be lived. Do I follow the truth or cover things up with more lies? One thing was true: I loved her. My love for Le'Chelle, for many years, was about what I could get. Something was changing. I was starting to feel something new about love—about what I could *give*, not what I could take, in this relationship. If it was a matter of convenience, it would have been just this cover-up. But I couldn't do that. I knew other people who suggested it, who were close in proximity. And I know because of Jesus in the freedom He gave me and the Father's love for me. I didn't want to live the lie anymore. I just didn't want to do that. It was a real battle coming freshly into faith, this whole new experience. People didn't know how I was playing this game. I had enough truth. I had to start facing my lies. I had to confess. I really loved her. Could I love this boy or girl, whatever this child would be? I already did.

After the Fiesta Bowl national championship game victory over the Miami Hurricanes, I was headed to Japan for the Japan Bowl, so I didn't talk to Le'Chelle for what felt like a couple of weeks. She had no idea what I was thinking about the situation, and I had no idea what she was thinking. The whole time, a wrestling match was going on inside me. After getting back from Japan, I talked to one of the pastors at the church that was now discipling me, and he simply asked, "Do you love her?" When he asked me that, it got real. I love this woman. No matter what happened, I wanted to be with her. Baby or no baby, I wanted to be with her. Having a baby made it even more important because I wanted to take responsibility. This was a part of me becoming a man, taking responsibility and not abandoning her. I never wanted to hurt her. "Yes," I replied. There was never a question about me loving Le'Chelle. In my heart of hearts there had never been anyone else.

At that moment, it became clear what to do. I called her and said, "I want to marry you." Le'Chelle hesitated because she didn't know how sincere I was, if this was some sort of move out of guilt or obligation. "I'm going to spend the rest of my life with you and be a good father to our child," I told her. What I discovered was Le'Chelle had already made plans to keep the baby. Abortion was never even a micro thought for her. She and her cousin were planning to raise our child without me. At Florida State they were going to schedule their classes around who was going to watch the baby at what time. Le'Chelle had decided to move on without me.

A Deep-Breath Moment

Now she was considering my proposal. Before she answered, however, I had to confess everything to her. I understood now that I was loved by Jesus in my mess, in my shame, in my pain, in my rejection, and all of that. I was loved. Though I had nothing about me that was lovable, He loved me. My heart started to love Jesus too. That was just a response. I was loving a God that I didn't even really know yet because of what He was doing for me, how He was changing some things in me. I had to start facing what my decision was going to be, what move I was about to make. I could go back to the convenience of darkness, be cool with it. Or I could face it with the little bit of truth I had. I did the latter.

Part of living in this truth now, this new way of life, was I loved her. I became committed to her. I wanted to marry her. The obvious question from Le'Chelle was, "Are you doing this out of convenience? Are you doing this because you have to?" That was one of the victories I had in the midst of a lot of complicated stuff; I decided to tell the truth. This time I get to tell the truth. I was able to say to her, "I love you, because I want to spend the rest of my life with you." That was actually the truth. I believe God impressed upon my heart for me to marry her. I was able to tell her the truth.

That was a real "deep-breath moment" for me. Now I was about to find out if I really believed in the truth as a new way of life, or if it was something that helped me out for a few moments, and then I could go back to my lies. It was like a crossroads. I needed to pick one direction or the other. I knew I had to tell Le'Chelle, "All those things you heard about me in high school and at Penn State, all those things were true. I lived a lie." I'd rather feel the pain than see Le'Chelle in pain ever. It was one of the hardest days of my life, to have to tell her the truth about *this girl* and *that girl* and *being there*, and there are no words to describe the pain I put her in. It was killing me. I can't measure my feelings against hers. I wouldn't dare, because my heart wasn't hard anymore. I was becoming a human being with a heart that was changed by the truth.

In saying and speaking the truth to her, every word was painful. There were a lot of words, so there was a lot of pain. She was stunned at first. Then she would ask me questions. I felt as though my breath were being taken away again. Have mercy, the pain was almost unbearable. To see her broken, her feeling taken advantage of, and her dignity stripped was almost unbearable. But Jesus found me, and He started telling me, "Hey, you *were* that; now let Me show you who you're supposed to be." I had wanted that all my life. That's what I wanted. I didn't know it was gonna be so painful to find out. Seeing that woman in pain made me hate the lies that I believed. This conversation was killing me, and I was killing everything I loved. It was a knife to my soul seeing the reality of myself, that I had been the man I did not want my mother to be with. Repeating the cycle of my earthly father had turned me into him, even though I never knew him. Faced with this reality, this was my world right now. Rehearsing this over and over again, somehow she saw that I actually was telling the truth for the first time. I think that's where the hope was. She was thinking, "If you're going to tell me this, you must be different. Something must be different in you." She knew I could live my whole married life, and she would never know. She chose to believe me, though it would be a while before she could trust me. It was only through Jesus paying the penalty for my sins and giving me the gift of forgiveness and new life that the cycle could be broken. It was in the process of being broken. Le'Chelle forgave me through all the pain and because she did love me too. She said, "Yes. We'll get married, but there's still some healing that needs to take place."

We ended up having a small wedding ceremony on February 28, 1987, at a museum in Tallahassee. I hitched a ride with some friends who every year went down to Florida for a fishing trip. They dropped me off on their way down and picked me up on their way back. Oh, D.J. came along too. He was by my side, supporting Le'Chelle and me. I have to tell what D.J. said in an interview for this book about this time. "You were getting ready to graduate, head to the pros, and then have to deal with this in the middle of a championship game. You made a man decision without a man in your life. For you to make that decision, no matter what the other options were, you made the right decision. You were willing to face whatever you needed to face, and decided to move forward from there. So that wedding was amazing. Because, like you now know, I knew more than you thought I knew. Watching you go through it and then come out right. I'm talking about doing the right thing and being in the right place at the right time. Everything that we did God orchestrated. I'm not saying everything we decided on the evil side. But God had His hand in our being roommates. That was orchestrated; that was not an accident. It's crazy when you look at the timing. And obviously, you found the right woman." Thank you, D.J.

With our child growing inside her, Le'Chelle would finish that semester at Florida State and then move up to Penn State to be with me. At this point, I need to go back a bit and talk about Le'Chelle's experience with the Holy Spirit while at Florida State. When I experienced the supernatural gift of speaking in tongues, I told her about it. D.J.'s youth pastor, who prayed for me, prayed for her over the phone, and she experienced the power of God over the phone. It was during a time when her roommates were out and Le'Chelle was in the room. She was being ministered to and abruptly her roommates burst into the room to find her sitting on the floor, bawling. Le'Chelle was speaking in tongues, and their minds were blown. Her cousin had grown up in a religion that believed you had to tarry and do all these exercises, and if you didn't do enough, you wouldn't be able to receive the spiritual gift of speaking in tongues. Because she never received that gift, she thought God had rejected her and didn't love her. She left God and started living in the world. When she saw what happened to Le'Chelle, it blew her mind and eventually, she came back to the Lord too. Le'Chelle's life was transformed by the power of the Holy Spirit, and she would never be the same. The two of us would become a team.

NO ONE GETS OUT OF THE BOAT

I remember our conversations early on, Le'Chelle and I saying, "No matter what, no one gets out of the boat." We both came from different worlds. She had a father, but her mom and dad had gotten divorced. I had never even seen my father. So we knew whatever remnant of sin, patterns of dysfunction, and things like that, we just wanted to see them broken. We believed it was the Father's plan to break that, but we had to participate. I had football, but now I was a husband too. I have never done that before. So we had the motto "No one gets out of the boat." We might be on other sides of the boat at times, but no one gets out. No matter what it takes, we're going to walk this out. We're not going to use certain words, such as divorce. It's easy to celebrate good times, but how are we going to survive the bad times and the challenges? We built boundaries. So she didn't leave when I bought her a billy goat coat. That actually happened. I was thinking, "I'm really blessed with my wife." I went to Burlington Coat Factory and was ready to do it big. I bought her a coat, but it was a billy goat coat. I didn't have a daddy to tell me, "Boy! What are you doing? You don't buy pots and pans for her birthday or Christmas present." The first year we were married, I bought Le'Chelle workout equipment and pots and pans. That was the dumbest thing ever. As for the billy goat coat, she wore it once. She actually did. She was being gracious. There were things I was trying to figure out as well, such as how to be a husband, and soon how to be a dad.

I got drafted by the Pittsburgh Steelers, which was another way the Father was guiding when I didn't know it. Of all the thirty-two teams I could have gone to, what are the odds? We were able to stay in Pennsylvania for a good while, which you'll see later would be critical to my foundational development into a man of God, husband, and father. I had a few months before reporting to training camp in Latrobe, Pennsylvania, only about a hundred miles from Centre Hall, Pennsylvania, where we were staying.

A wonderful couple, Gary and Becky Ream, let us live with them. Gary was a co-owner of and ran Woodward Camp. Becky was pregnant too, so she and Le'Chelle were pregnant together, which was kind of cool. I had met Gary through a teammate, Mike Stillman, whose dad was also an investment businessman who was co-owner of Woodward. We used to go to the Reams' house on the weekends and eat steaks and snow crabs and have a blast. They were a safe place, a family for us when we didn't have our biological families. And we worked for the camp in the summers to have extra money, including working an entire summer for the nice Schwinn bike that became my only means of transportation around campus. Gary and Becky were great friends to us; they took us in. Le'Chelle worked for the Reams at Woodward Camp and made two hundred dollars a week while living with them in Centre Hall, forty-five minutes from the camp. I had to spend my days physically preparing for the upcoming Steelers training camp in Latrobe. Centre Hall was the perfect place for us to be so I could train and prep until we could get a place of our own in Pittsburgh after I made the team... *if* I made the team.

CHAPTER 9

PREPARE TO LEAVE

For a moment before we go any further, let's recap, just to put things into perspective. It was spring of 1987, and I was a new and growing believer. Jesus had given me a divine encounter of love that changed everything. It completely rerouted the pursuits of my life. "Pursue *this* love," He had said. That was my new plumb line for life. In February of that year, after following a directive from the Holy Spirit confirming my deep love, Le'Chelle and I were married. I was trying to figure out how to love her the way the Father would have me to. She was pregnant, and I was about to be a father—a fatherless man becoming a father. Eventually, the Father would reveal Himself to me in yet another profound way that let me know He had been there all along and would be there guiding me in the future. The Pittsburgh Steelers had drafted me, and I was in intensive pre-camp training. With a family now, my motivation for making the team and securing a solid contract had shifted. Some of that internal furniture was being moved around. I was no longer living for me. My life now was about something bigger than Tim Johnson.

The emotion and pressure were also on a new level, yet so was the peace. It's amazing that we can have pressure squeezing us from multiple directions and still have assurance and comfort. One of the apostles in the Bible days, Paul, wrote, "We are hard pressed on every side, but not crushed; perplexed, but not in despair" (2 Cor. 4:8). I was certainly pressed and perplexed but never crushed or in despair. That's something only the Father can do, even if you are young in the faith and lacking Bible knowledge, even if your theology is not perfectly correct. The Father's love is greater.

Le'Chelle arrived in May, and the baby was due in August. We were living with Gary and Becky in a little suburb outside of State College. Since Le'Chelle was working at the Woodward Camp making two hundred dollars a week and I couldn't work because of being in training, thankfully, the Reams graciously didn't charge us for rent or anything. God sent them at a critical time to help us through that period. That's what He does. He sends us people. I did get a small signing bonus for training camp. That was enough for me to purchase a desperately needed vehicle, but that was about it. I would have to make the team before being offered a significant contract. (I signed a contract with a small bonus to get a car but wouldn't get paid the salary for the year unless I made the team.)

I HAD BEEN A PART OF TWO NATIONAL CHAMPIONSHIPS AND EVENTUALLY WOULD GO TO THE SUPER BOWL AND WIN IT ALL.... BUT NONE OF THE FEELINGS I HAD THEN CAME CLOSE TO THE EMOTIONS RUNNING THROUGH ME WHEN I LOOKED INTO MY BABY GIRL'S EYES FOR THE FIRST TIME.

In July I headed off to camp in Latrobe, and we only had two short breaks during the training. Being away from my wife that long with the baby coming was challenging. My mind was divided, and being the best required incredible focus and study. Remember, I was trying to make the team, which ain't easy. The jump from high school to college had been intense, but the jump from college to professional was intense on steroids. Despite being in the best shape of my life and training harder than I had ever trained, I still had to push myself beyond my perceived limits just to hopefully make the cut.

Right in the middle of training camp on a humid August day, I got the call that Le'Chelle was going into labor. Now, leaving training camp was not something recommended for players needing to make the cut. Believe me, the moment you are absent, someone is right there waiting in the wings, ready to step up and take your spot. Well aware of this, there was still no way I was going to miss the birth of my child—no way. My defensive line coach, Joe Greene, as in the one-and-only Mean Joe Greene, let me go. Without the slightest hesitation, I jumped in my car and drove off. The Father is my witness here. I do not know how I made it to the hospital. Exhausted and alone, running on fumes, I believe I was asleep for a good chunk of the drive. There were sections that were blank, as if I were in a trance or something. It looked bad for me to be this out of it. I was about to have my first child. Once I was at the hospital, try and picture this six-foot-three-inch, 275-pound NFL defensive lineman rushing through the corridors, trying to find his laboring wife's room. Let's just say heads turned. Though I was this massive athlete, that tiny baby girl was about to bring me to my knees quicker than any opponent on the field could.

When Christa was born, everything inside me shuttered. There are no words to adequately describe the emotion of seeing her come into this world. I had been a part of two national championships and eventually would go to the Super Bowl and win it all. The confetti would fall, and the championship rings slipped on my finger. But none of the feelings I had then came close to the emotions running through me when I looked into my baby girl's eyes for the first time. Our first daughter—she's the one who made me a father. With a thousand conflicting thoughts shooting through my mind like flaming arrows, I felt the weight of responsibility for this innocent being, who is completely dependent on her mother and me. I felt the weight of the power of influence I would have in her life.

Then, fear tried to creep in. "What if I let her down?" I said to myself. "What if I fail? Not sure if I can do this. I don't know if I can raise a child." My father walked away from me when I was a baby, and I'd seen men not treat my mom well. I knew the things that were inside of them, what they were capable of. I knew what was inside me. I've had coaches, great coaches. I had the influence of godly men in my life, but when you're suddenly a father, it's different. The questions were endless, and the void was huge.

As I held tiny Christa in my arms and looked down into her sparkling eyes that were gazing back at me, I'd never seen anything so beautiful, so tender. Kissing her forehead, and taking in the sweet scent of her soft skin, I swelled with love for her in the most helpless state she was in. And even in the midst of all the questions and the fear of not knowing, there was no way I was ever going to not give everything I had. I had to learn how to be the father I never had. A child without a father feels like a mistake. I determined right then and there Christa would never feel that. I was ready to grow and learn. When every one of my children was born, each was a unique experience of a lifetime. And there are all kinds of amazing stories behind those, but the first one shakes you like no other.

Though I knew how to take on a fullback head-on, I had no idea how to take this on. I was scared. Nevertheless, that quiet inner calm was there affirming me, "Trust Me. I've got this." As I recalled my experience at the table and the words "Pursue *this* love," I felt the greatest hope I'd ever felt. Without a doubt, this was going to be a test. It was bigger than me. In fact, bigger than me seemed to be the theme of my life. The Father was going to have to show up in various ways and places, or I was going to be dead meat.

And He would show up in the most powerful way. Not only was the Father going to father me, but He would show me how to be a father.

Even with everything revolving around being a new husband and father, being drafted by the NFL was a huge opportunity for me and my young family. This was something I had worked hard for since those days at Ringling Redskins Park. Like millions of other kids, growing up, I'd idolized my sports heroes and pretended to be them when playing in the yard, perhaps in the back of my mind dreaming of one day being a pro too. The hard fact, however, is not even 1 percent of young dreamers ever get the chance to do what I was doing. I was well aware of that fact as I walked around the Steelers facility in awe. And when I slipped that Steelers helmet on for the first time, it was almost out-of-body. To think I, Timothy Johnson, from the lower-income side of Sarasota, Florida, was now sharing a locker room with Hall of Fame legends Mike Webster, John Stallworth, Donnie Shell, Tony Dungy, Coach Chuck Noll, and Mean Joe Greene, who was also one of my coaches. These guys were legends. I mean, the Steelers owned the '70s. I came from being at the highest level of college football, was a Walter Camp All American, a national champion. Now, walking into those quarters, all that meant nothing. Pro football has only one thing in common with every other football level: the term *football*. But it's even a totally different kind of football.

Now, Mean Joe was my defensive line coach. Remember him? First of all, he's a legend. A Hall of Famer. Probably the best, most dominant defensive lineman I've ever watched footage of. He was also featured in a wildly popular Coca-Cola commercial. In it, in a stadium walkway, where Mean Joe was limping after a hard-fought game, a young boy gives him his ice-cold bottle of Coke. Mean Joe downs the bottle in one massive swallow. He walks off, then turns around and says, "Hey, kid?" At that, Mean Joe tosses the boy his sweaty jersey. Classic. Tony Dungy was the defensive back coach, and Mean Joe Greene was a rookie coach. I tell people we were rookies together. He was a rookie coach, and I was a rookie player. While the experience of it all was mind-blowing, it didn't take long for me to come back down to earth. This was indeed the NFL, the best of the best, and these guys were lighting it up on a stratospheric level. And as a sixth-round draft choice on the bubble, I still had to make the team.

Joe Greene was such a kind man until something didn't happen that needed to happen. At the first meeting in training camp, he told us, "I'm not going to cut anybody." I was thinking, "One second. There are at least eight or nine guys here. You can only keep seven." I was calculating this in my head. How was this going to happen? Then he said, "You're going to cut yourself for how you treat this opportunity. But if you do everything that I say to do, I'll find a way to keep you." That's all I needed to know. That's all. I knew I was not going to be the smartest or the most talented, but I would outwork everybody. That was my ticket in with the team. That was my edge.

Training camp was harder than I thought it would be. Everybody was big, moving fast, and strong. Early on I remember feeling so lost because I was a couple of steps behind the other guys I was competing with. In the NFL a couple of steps is huge because everything is moving so fast, and the margin of error is razor thin. Everybody was just as big and strong as I was, if not bigger and stronger. In college I played on the right side of the defensive line with my right hand down. To my surprise, the Steelers kept me on the right side but switched me to the left hand down on the line. That's a huge deal because now I had to play with a whole different body movement, which is not a problem for guys who have a lot of athleticism, but it didn't come so easy for me, and it affected how I exploded off the line of scrimmage into the offensive lineman on the cutoff block and the reach block. Those milliseconds lost are the difference between success and failure. I was really struggling and couldn't get it with my left hand down, and the guy I was up against was eating my lunch.

One day in the middle of practice, I just gave up. "I can't do this," I said. "I just can't do it." In my mind I was trying to figure out how I was going to survive when Joe saw what was happening and graciously pulled me aside. "It's gonna be OK, Tim," he said, and then he began working with me on my steps. To this day I'm forever grateful for that man. He saw something in me, and the message he gave me was, "Don't lose what you've got. You know how to do the cutoff block. It feels awkward at first because your left hand's down, but we're gonna get this. Just keep at it." Joe Greene worked repetitious drill work with me until I got it right. "If you do everything I say," he told me, "you'll be fine and make the cut." I'm extreme. So you know, I ended up pushing myself above and beyond the call of duty. I worked my tail off and learned how to play the reach block with my left hand down. After that it was on and popping! I got trained by the best.

I was working harder than anybody when I got the call and had to leave training camp. I couldn't afford to miss a day, but I had a wife and a baby coming. After all, I was looking for this to be my job. I had some awareness that football isn't everything, and I did have a marketing job offer in Chicago because I had gotten my degree in four years. The Father had other plans, though.

The next day, while I was at the hospital with Le'Chelle and

Christa, Gary came into the room and said, "Tim made the team." I said, "What? I made the team?"

"Yes, you did," said Gary. "I got a call from Joe Greene. He asked about you." We didn't have cell phones back then, and Gary, being astute and insightful, took that personal call at the house from Mean Joe Greene asking about Le'Chelle, the baby, and me—and of course relaying the news that I had made the cut.

"I guess it's not over, then!" I said, brimming with excitement and not knowing quite how to respond. "I got to go back and go to war. There are more battles to fight." That was a very formative time for me, learning how to go to the highest level of whatever the Father planned for me. His will was tested, and I passed a lot of tests. This was the highest level of testing because it took so much to not only meet there but be sustained there.

Joe Greene forever holds a special place in my heart for all he did for me. The hand of the Father put one of the best to ever play the game into my life. Joe meant what he said, because I did everything he said, and I made the team. I wound up getting a decent contract. It wasn't like the big ones I would eventually get, but it was adequate to live on and raise a family. We moved to Pittsburgh, and I became immersed in the NFL and family life.

One day I was walking through the locker room, taking everything in, and I heard the Father whisper something to me. It was that still, small voice that I have now come to recognize as the Holy Spirit. The Father, the Son, and the Holy Spirit are one. Resonating from deep inside my soul, I couldn't ignore it. He said, "I'm going to father you. I want you to build a life in my Son, not in the NFL." The instruction was clear, and what I understood it to mean was, "Don't build your life based on the way this world wants you to live, because of a title; live for My Son, Jesus, in the NFL. Let that be your identity." Then, the Holy Spirit's words reverberated, "Prepare to leave." I knew that didn't come from me because I was just coming into the game and was all fired up. It had to be from the Father. But what did that mean? He wasn't telling me to leave that instant but prepare to leave. The way forward for me was to live for Him, preparing to leave the game as I was coming in. In other words, "Work hard, do your best, enjoy it as much as possible, but hold it loosely. Always be ready to lay it down so that nothing becomes greater than life in My Son.

As time progressed, I understood that everything I was doing in preparing to leave the game I loved brought more meaning to me being in it. Some guys go in never wanting to leave and can't lay it down when it's time to. The game can have a grip on you. Your whole identity can be in the NFL, so when you are forced out, some guys go into deep depression or don't know how to function because their identity is gone. This mindset of preparing to leave and not getting caught up in all the accolades kept me grounded. I believe this is how the Father wants us to hold everything in life.

CHAPTER 10

I'M THE FIRST MIRACLE
I'VE EVER SEEN

At this point, we were living in Pittsburgh in a small town-house, and I was making an average rookie salary for a sixth-rounder. Again, not the big money, but enough to adequately support my family while developing my playing skills, building my value. During my rookie year the Father continued growing me and revealing more of Himself in unique and supernatural ways. I was learning what it means to be a true disciple of Jesus and a godly husband and father, while negotiating my way through the NFL God's way. The Holy Spirit of Jesus had begun the process of sculpting me into His image. That's a process that starts the moment we receive His life and continues until the day we take in our last breath and see Him face-to-face. He teaches us in bits and pieces, "precept upon precept; line upon line, line upon line; here a little, and there a little" (Isa. 28:10, KJV).

On the journey of becoming the man God intends for me to be, so many times Le'Chelle has been the tool in His hands. Of course, all the male influences in my life have been great and used of God, but there's nothing like being in closed quarters and having your insecurities exposed to someone who loves you enough to deal with you through the good and the ugly. The fans in the stands were seeing the big tackles and quarterback sacks, while Le'Chelle was seeing the emotional and often immature boy who would emerge from inside the helmet and under the shoulder pads.

I used to get offended when she wouldn't automatically agree with my opinions, that she had her own ideas about the way things should be done. While she loved and supported me, she didn't stroke my ego when she saw things a bit differently. Le'Chelle certainly wasn't perfect, but she had a direct line to God and had wisdom. I tell people I've heard the voice of God, and many times it sounds a lot like my wife's! When I got offended and all up in my feelings, my underlying issues with anger would get exposed. I didn't explode in rage, but I would be mad if things didn't go my way and would sulk, exposing my insecurities.

One night after getting into an argument, I grabbed my Bible and headed to the couch. In my mind there was no question that I was right, and I was going to prove it by reading the Bible. I flipped open the Bible, and it opened to Isaiah 57:21, which says, "'There is no peace,' says my God, 'for the wicked.'" The word *wicked* leaped off the page into my heart. I was being *wicked*. While not audible, the voice of the Holy Spirit was unmistakable and convicting. It struck me so deeply that I rushed back to Le'Chelle in the other room, humbled myself, and apologized. I never slept on a couch again.

Our marriage, really any godly marriage, is more than simply being together as a couple. The Father had a divine plan that involved both of us. When we truly became one and valued each other, a seed was conceived, and God was growing something that required both of us to bring it to full term and birth. I needed Le'Chelle to help me become the man God wanted me to be, and she needed me to help her become the woman God wanted her to be. One can put a thousand to flight, but two, ten thousand (Deut. 32:30). The enemy of our souls knows that relationships have this value and power, so all hell is unleashed against them. Marriage is more than just for our happiness and pleasure, which is wonderful; it's about our growth.

When it came to parenting, the same was true. Being first-time parents of a newborn was challenging for both Le'Chelle and me. Yet God showed up in amazing ways, teaching us and letting us know He was on the scene.

AN ANGEL RESCUE

We even had an authentic angel visitation. There is really no other explanation. It was a picture of the Father fathering me and showing me how to father my daughter when I had no access to help her. Jill, Le'Chelle's cousin, was living with us at the time and helping out. Christa had some problems sleeping, and because we were new parents, we didn't know about sleep training or have all the knowledge that's available today. We knew there was a practice of letting the baby cry, and then, if it gets to be too much, going to get the baby, and repeating that. We had been working on that, and it was hard. One particular night while I was on the road playing a game somewhere, Christa went into an unusually intense crying spell. Le'Chelle woke up and was about to go get her in the other room when Christa suddenly became quiet. The extreme crying just stopped instantly. Le'Chelle was lying in bed and rolled over. When she did, someone handed her Christa. The lights were out, so it was dark. Le'Chelle assumed it was Jill.

The next morning, Christa was still in the bed with Le'Chelle when Jill came in and jokingly said, "I'm going to tell Tim you let Christa sleep in the bed." Le'Chelle's face contorted. "Well," she said, "you brought her to me."

"No," Jill said, puzzled, "I didn't. I didn't bring you Christa."

"Stand up right there," Le'Chelle said. She had Jill stand up next to the bed, and then she realized it couldn't have been Jill because of how big the torso was of the person who handed her Christa. No one else was in the house. Christa wasn't even a year old, so she couldn't walk. Though not far away, she was in the other room; you had to walk to get there. It had to have been an angel that comforted Christa and brought her to her mother. Le'Chelle and Jill just sat there a while in awe, with no words. Le'Chelle said, "I remember seeing knees." She was in and out of sleep, but she remembered seeing the knees and torso of the person handing Christa to her while I was away. When the Father said He was going to father me, He would do stuff like that, absolutely supernatural. You cannot explain it.

Later on, the reason for the crying became evident. There were times we players would go do events for community organizations, such as raise money. We were caravanning to an event, and one of my teammates' mothers was riding with him. I remember driving up next to them and her looking out the window. When she did, I saw a demon in her face and backed off. I never said anything to anybody. Before that, she had given us some dolls to give to Christa. You know where those dolls were? In my daughter's room next to her bed. Witchcraft! It was the Father fathering me. We had been clueless as to why she was screaming the way she was. The child was being tormented. The Holy Spirit said, "Take those dolls out." I would not have known otherwise. The angel rescued her because she was screaming. I got home, took the dolls out of her room, and then put them in the garbage to go out the next day. We never had a problem like that again. Never.

THE FLOOR

I had played the '87 season, and now it was the '88 offseason. This was a couple of years after my table experience back at State College, in '86. It was right afterward that D.J. and I got connected to Unity Christian Fellowship and several of their mature men of God, leaders in the church, had begun discipling us. We were young and passionate, soaking up their teaching like dry sponges. After that, getting drafted and moving to Pittsburgh was a God thing in itself. Out of all the NFL teams I could have been drafted to, I went there, and it allowed me to stay connected to my church during a critical period of my development. During my rookie season I did Bible studies with teammates, but as soon as the offseason hit, Le'Chelle and I would drive from Pittsburgh up to Penn State on the weekends for church and leadership training and then turn around and drive back. It was three and a half hours one way. I would do training during the week, and when Friday evening came, we'd pack Christa and some food in the car and hit the road, full of joy the whole way. Le'Chelle and I just couldn't believe this new life we had in Christ. We would've driven to California and back if it was required. Driving three and a half hours one way wasn't nothing; it was the joy of our lives. I was so hungry and needy to grow and to learn, and to maximize what this was supposed to be.

We'd get there Friday night, start fellowshipping, and then attend leadership meetings on Saturday morning. Our pastor led the group. After spending time as a group in prayer and worship, we'd have a lesson and other ministry activities throughout the day. On Sunday morning we'd go to church, then get in the car and head back to Pittsburgh for my training during the week. This was our regular routine, every single weekend. On one of those routine weekends, however, the Father had another surprise encounter waiting for me.

We had arrived on Friday, as usual. Saturday morning came, and we were all gathered in a circle, praying with the pastor as we'd been doing for weeks, when out of nowhere I was on the floor, bawling like I'd never bawled before. I'm talking *heaving crying*, in the fetal position, wailing, and no one knowing what to do. I was very embarrassed but couldn't stop. I was wondering, "What in the world is going on here? Why are you on the floor? What's wrong with you? God, what are You telling me here?" Back then, I had some muscles, so it must have been quite a spectacle, this mammoth NFL player on the floor, crying his eyes out like a baby. I'm sure it made some of the people around me uncomfortable, but I couldn't stop.

What was happening was bigger than me.

"GOD SAYS HE IS GOING TO FATHER YOU." WITH THOSE SIMPLE WORDS CAME A SUPERNATURAL PEACE THAT PASSES ALL UNDERSTANDING AND A QUIET CONFIDENCE THAT SETTLED OVER ME. SINCE THAT DAY, BACK IN 1988, THE FATHER HAS FATHERED ME....I WAS *FATHERLESS* NO MORE.

Eventually, my pastor inched over gingerly. I barely saw his blurry form out of the corner of my eye, but I felt his presence. "Everything OK?" he spoke in a low, gentle voice. He didn't know what to do with me. No one knew. *I* didn't know. The weeping eventually waned to slow breaths, and I was lying there in a puddle of my own drool. Then, as quickly as I had dropped to the floor, it was as if a light switch had flipped on in my head. Introspection came, and then illumination, Holy Spirit illumination. "I've never had a father. Oh, never had a father. I never had a father!" Everything exploded again. The weeping, the shaking, and I didn't know where it was all coming from. I didn't know. Whatever pain was buried deep inside me my whole life had erupted. This went on for some time. Those around me recognized God was doing something and let me lie there. After however long it was—ten minutes or ten hours; it didn't matter, for time was irrelevant—the pastor said to me, "God says He is going to father you." With those simple words came a supernatural peace that passes all understanding and a quiet confidence that settled over me. Since that day, back in 1988, the Father has fathered me.

This was a revelation that had to come directly from the Father. The leadership at the church, or anywhere, for that matter, couldn't teach me this. It had to be encountered. Jesus Himself, no human origin, was a part of this. He Himself, as His Son, introduced me to the Father. What I realized is Jesus saved me to introduce me to the Father. Since I didn't have an earthly father, He didn't leave me an orphan. He introduced me to Himself as my Lord, as my Redeemer, and as the One I belong to. He taught me how to believe, and that has affected my behavior, because I've received His love and I love Him. He's all I have. And He's put people in my life, surrogate fathers and mothers, spiritual fathers, men who have mentored me and coached me. Everyone along the way has been a gift to me. He put so many gifts in my life, but the Father is the source of those gifts.

At that moment on the floor, the cycle was broken.

I was no longer bound by my fatherlessness.

Knowing I'm loved by the Father and that He is fathering me gave me a sense of security and confidence that whatever He says about me, whatever He sees, is the way it is, regardless of how I see myself or feel. I've had to grow in that understanding—I'm still growing in it—but there's nothing like it. So the pressure of having to be shaped or being conformed by a cultural paradigm or idea, or the pressure of what people say or do, was relieved in a measure because I no longer needed that. Now I realized that all those days since being a kid knowing there's something more, that I'm really *not a mistake*, that there's something bigger, knowing who I am and where I am going—all those questions all those years were answered in one encounter.

He's my father, He loves me, and He's going to father me. He's the help when I feel helpless. He's near when I have nobody to call. He's the hope when I feel at the end of my rope. He's everything I was looking for all my life. It has affected me by believing I can live a life I've never seen before. I didn't see this growing up. I tell people, "I'm the first miracle I've ever seen. You can argue with my doctrine and what I believe, but you cannot argue with my story. *I'm the first miracle I've ever seen.* The Father, through Jesus and the Holy Spirit, was guiding me and teaching me how to love. I was to love my wife as Christ loved the church, dying for her and stooping down to wash her feet. I now viewed my coaches and team-mates differently, with compassion. When my eyes fell upon Christa (and each child after her), unlike my earthly father, who had turned and walked away, I was filled with this awe and wonder and holy responsibility not only to be a good earthly father but to lead them to the good, good Father.

Upon reflection of that encounter on the floor, one of the things I realized was how common it was to every man and woman who has experienced fatherlessness and has denied it. They suppressed it and gave up on the idea, developing a whole life without a desire or need for that. I didn't realize how much I had covered up until it was revealed and exposed on that floor by supernatural grace, the grace of Jesus. You can delay your need for a father, but you will never be able to deny it. Leading into the confrontation of when I really was with my earthly father, all the things that I had stuffed, buried, and avoided, and didn't want to need, popped up on the floor that day like a beach ball pushed underwater. The pressure had been building up. I think the stage was set for the Father to give me a chance to trust Him. By again letting go of all the stuff I had held on to, I actually experienced the love of God. Interestingly, I didn't even know I was holding on to the fact that I never had a father. It was affecting me, but I didn't realize it. So the amazing love of God met me there. At the appointed time, I had that moment of breakthrough, break-down, transformation, whatever you want to call it. I admitted and confessed what I was missing. I burst out because of what I had experienced. In the love of God, I was willing to let go now. The thought I had was that we human beings who have been fatherless and who have been orphans in our thinking, orphans in our behavior, never feeling at home, feeling alone, not being secure, not having a sense of safety, not having a sense of truly belonging—all that was there was answered in one moment. When we burst out, we can burst out into healing, or we're going to burst out into more destruction.

In working over the years with individuals, I know that eventually everyone is going to burst out. You can only hold that beach ball down so long before it manifests in a way that allows one to be delivered. It allowed me to be honest, to express what was in me. I was healed. I was absolutely healed. What happens when a man has to express this? Anger is going to come out, even fear, revenge, adultery, fornication—any lifestyle he wants to live just comes out. But it doesn't heal. You live however you want, but is that going to heal you eter-nally? Is that going to heal the deepest part of our beings? I don't think so because a broken vessel can't heal itself. Just because I do things that make me feel good doesn't mean I'm healed. It just means I've covered it up pretty well. I've allowed my strength to overcome my weaknesses. At the end of the day, however, all our weaknesses will deplete our strength, and that's when we become vulnerable. Early on in life, it hap-pened to me. Then, it was accelerated, and I got to that place. There is a time in all our lives when we're going to have to face the reality of something missing on the inside, relationally, that we didn't get from our earthly fathers.

Even if it takes you sixty, seventy years, you will come to the place where a roar comes out of you. But without Jesus it is going to be anger, compulsive behavior, greed, pride, bitterness. It's going to be rage and violence. All the false attachments and identities that are the effects of fatherlessness because you denied it, will explode out of you. Then, there's the flip side. Because you know you *do* need it and *have* cared about it, you've been lost without that place of a father speaking into you and you're experiencing the same effects as those who have suppressed it. You can delay your need for the Father. But you will never be able to deny it. Something is coming out of you that expresses the pain. At some point it will erupt. The question is, Will you have a Healer showing you His love and introducing you to the Father who is the only One that can free you from the effects of what you didn't have? That is absolutely the truth, whichever side you represent. For me, the question was answered. I was *fatherless no more.*

CHAPTER 11

"CLEAN IT UP"

I would be in Pittsburgh for three years. One day during my rookie year at training camp at Saint Vincent College in Latrobe, I was in the locker room after practice, ready to bolt out of there to go to dinner. You would come out of the locker room, and Steelers fans were everywhere. It was packed. You could have been the least-known guy on the team, but everybody wanted your autograph. I was signing autographs every day. It was great. This is when the Father made a strong point with me. He knew what He had delivered me from through the sacrifice of His Son, Jesus. He didn't want me to go back to anything other than knowing *He is there for me, He sees me, I belong to Him, and my life matters.* The Father, through the Holy Spirit, started speaking to my heart. It was a voice I was learning to recognize and that was becoming clearer as I grew in Him. "Clean it up," He said, and I instinctively knew what that meant. He wasn't saying, "Clean up your locker," but, "Clean up the locker room, all of it." It was a small college, so it wasn't like our NFL locker room or the facilities at major universities today. It wasn't the nicest of places. We would come in after practice as dirty as can be after smashing into one another for a couple of hours on the field, and all the grass, dirt, mud, and ripped-off tape from practicing all day was in the shower area. The small shower area was open, and there was a large gray garbage can in that space. Everything would be right there on the old tile floor, with little puddles of mud from the dirt mixing with the water leaking from the shower area; that area gave us the heebie-jeebies. When I heard, "Clean it up," I thought, "Hang on, we have people to do this. We actually pay people to do this."

"I am fathering you so that your image won't be as a celebrity in the NFL but that of My Son."

At that, I decided to wait for all the guys to leave, and then clean up the locker room. I remember thinking, "Whatever You desire me to do. Oh, Jesus, my answer is yes. What You've done for me, the price that I'm paying is *not* what it costs. It cost You far more than any little price I could pay to say thank you. It will take the rest of my life to thank you for what You did for me." This was a moment to express my love for Jesus and fellowship with my Father in the Holy Spirit privately. I would stay and clean it up. Then, I'd go out and sign autographs like everybody else. But the intimacy was developing. It wasn't about performance. It was about me learning how to be a son who was obedient to his Father and doing things that didn't benefit me but benefited other people. He was retraining me how to live for His kingdom and how to be free, even if it didn't make sense to other people. When the locker room cleared, I started picking up all the pieces of tape and other trash, and wet towels, leaving the locker room better than the way I found it. The whole time, the Father was talking to me. He was allowing me to die to the NFL while I was in the NFL. He was showing me Himself and how we were going to operate in this world. My love for Him was going to be service to other people. I would do anything for Jesus, to be close to Him, because only He could show me the Father. I don't always know how or what's going to happen, but the answer from me is *yes*.

I continued to work hard at my job as a defensive lineman

and got pretty good at it. Yet because the Father, not the world, was teaching me, I was able to keep things in perspective. One of the things I used to do on game days to help keep my priorities straight was write Colossians 3:23 on the tape on my wrist: "And whatever you do, do it heartily, as to the Lord and not to men" (NKJV). It was for me only, not public show. Whenever we do what we do heartily and enthusiastically for the Lord, not the approval of men, we work harder, and our reward comes from Him. I would write that scripture on my wrist to remind me that was building a life in Christ, not a life in the NFL. The complete passage reads, "And whatever you do, do it heartily, as to the Lord and not to men, knowing that from the Lord you will receive the reward of the inheritance; for you serve the Lord Christ" (Col. 3:23–24, NKJV). That scripture now defines my core in whatever I'm doing. It's not the *whatever* that defines me but the *who*. In sports, business, nursing, teaching, whatever occupation we choose, we can't look to the doing of it to define our being, because if we do, when we can't do that anymore, we become a lost speck on this piece of dirt moving through space and time.

"WHATEVER YOU DO, DO IT HEARTILY, AS TO THE LORD AND NOT TO MEN."

ON THE FLOOR AGAIN, BUT . . .

It was January 1990, after my third year with the Steelers—the '89 season had closed out, and then we crossed over into the new year. My contract was up, and I would soon be going into negotiation, something I'd never done before. I'd had a good three years, had started with decent numbers, was getting average pay, and was due a bump up. Now we were talking a new three-year contract worth a few million. I'd been faithful to my first contract, done my job, so I was feeling pretty good about things. Then, in January, I crawled out of bed one morning, took a step or two, and collapsed to the floor.

I was on the floor again, unable to move but in a different way than before. This time the tears welling up were not from the Father setting me free but from the searing physical pain. The experience was confusing because if you looked at me, on the surface everything appeared great and felt great. At six feet, three inches and now 280 pounds of muscle, I was a massive physical specimen. What could be wrong? Before I collapsed, there were no alarming issues that I was aware of. Long story short, I ended up in the hospital, and the level of pain in my body was off the charts. An average SED rate, which measures pain, may be 10 to 20. Mine was in the 80s. And the pain was constant and worse at night. In fact, it got so bad that I could not sleep in the bed, so I crashed in a hospital recliner or wheelchair. Still, a full night's sleep evaded me. Mind-numbingly painful, it was as if demons were running hot irons through my body. One night in the hospital I was trying desperately to find some relief, and I was on the side of the hospital bed, crying. The nurse came in, took one look at me, and said, "Why are you suffering like this?" Helpless and broken, I had no answers. The doctors were stumped too. After a week they released me on a ton of medication that would hopefully help manage what they still hadn't diagnosed.

The Steelers, mind you, have to know all about this. It went on my record, and I knew it would be held against me when contract negotiation time came. I was in what seemed an unavoidable disaster. I had a wife and kid—and oh, by the way, I needed my body for my work, and it wasn't working. Every night, my wife had to get out of the bed. I had to manage to get myself out of the bed so she could change all the sheets. Sweating wasn't even the word. We're talking pouring-out-like-a-waterfall sweat. The pain was so intense, and the sweat was flooding from my body. This went on for weeks, though they were doing everything they could. I finally got to where I could move around somewhat, but I was still in excruciating pain. I couldn't train, couldn't work out, couldn't condition, and that was a problem.

One day as I was hobbling to the training room, the trainer looked at me and said, "You know, this can be debilitating." In other words, "Your career could be over." That's pretty much what he was trying to say to me. I just looked back at him and didn't say a word. After a couple of months there was some improvement. I was able to swim and ride a bike, so I was training, riding up hills on the bike and swimming laps in the pool. Meanwhile, we were pushing toward summer, meaning camp was going to start in a few months, and all I could do was swim and bike. I couldn't even run. After speaking to my agent, I left with the strong impression that I had no leg to stand on in negotiations. Pun intended.

THE GOD WHO SEES

Now, here's where the Father supernaturally stepped in again, but we have to backpedal to 1989 for the total God setup. This is an amazingly miraculous event. About a year before my episode with what would officially be diagnosed as Reiter's syndrome, an autoimmune disease, Le'Chelle and I went with Todd Blackledge to a big prophetic conference in Kansas City. Todd Blackledge, the man who led me to Christ back at Penn State, left the Kansas City Chiefs, and we ended up becoming friends. He came to the Steelers my second year, and we became roommates on the road. Neither Le'Chelle nor I had been exposed to that level of prophetic ministry before. These guys were living in a different realm. At the conference they put us in these presbytery rooms, and we had appointments with the prophets who would come in and speak into our lives. Le'Chelle and I were sitting in the room, waiting, and she told me that she'd been repenting and clearing her heart. She said, "I don't want anything out here that may be shameful or embarrassing." She wasn't in some deep, dark sin or anything; she was just nervous. And maybe I was a little bit too, but actually I was more intrigued, wondering, "What is this going to be?"

They came in and spoke into my life first, and some of the stuff that I got prophetically in that room that day I'm still living out. It was amazing. They prophesied over me. One of the prophets looked at Le'Chelle and said, "Why do you wanna leave him?" Then he repeated, "Why do you wanna leave him?" Le'Chelle broke down and started bawling. No one knew, not even I, that she was planning to leave me. She was trying to figure out how to leave me. It wasn't because of any major marital dysfunction or her not loving me. The pressure was too great. She'd been up with the baby and a mother for the first time, and now she was out here where she was in a professional NFL environment with all the other wives. There was a lot going on spiritually, emotionally, and relationally, and I was just full of spiritual zeal with no wisdom. One day I went in to wake her up, and the Holy Spirit said, "Don't touch her." So I didn't. There was all this buildup, and then the prophet said, "Why do you wanna leave?" She was bawling. He continued, "I see you like a bucket that gets poured into, but there are holes. It's just all seeping out." And he adds, "The Lord is plugging up the holes. He's plugging up all the holes."

I was sitting there, wondering, "Huh? You were gonna leave me?" And it wasn't because of any ill intent.

She said, "I was trying to figure out how to just get back and go to my mama but realized, Tim ain't gonna let me take this baby. He's not gonna…" Le'Chelle was trying to figure out how to get from under all the weight she was carrying in her mind and heart. It wasn't that she didn't want to be with me; the pressure was too great.

Le'Chelle is gifted in so many ways. What I have to pray for hours for, she can do not even thinking. She is full of wisdom. In the early days of marriage our pastor spoke a word over Le'Chelle that the Father had a special relationship He wanted to have with her. I thought it was profound because this was early on, within the first year and a half of our marriage. That has been true. She has a love for God, and she also has this administrative, practical, pragmatic side of her. The fact that the Father spoke such great wisdom to her blew her mind. I think everything shifted in her from that moment. That prophetic word from God broke the heavy yoke and changed everything for us as a couple.

Because we were seeing the Father fathering us in so many ways like this, His presence in our lives became even more tangible. One of the prophets said to me, "The Lord is going to come to you in a dream, and He's going to come to you as the face of a friend."

"OK, that's a bit strange," I thought. "Wonder what the Father is up to?"

What is critical to get here is at this point I was feeling fine physically. It would be months later that I would have my episode and then enter into contract negotiations. We went back to Pittsburgh. Time passed. No dream featuring a friend as the prophet predicted had occurred. Reiter's syndrome hit, throwing my body into a tailspin right before my contract negotiations. Lo and behold, I have the dream just as prophesied, and in the dream it's my friend Todd Blackledge's face. Now stop right there. You can't make this stuff up or make it happen. Only God. Todd Blackledge's face was in a conversation with me. He said, "And this is what your contract is going to be." He gave me a three-year contract with the specific numbers, the amount for each year. And that dream carried me through the whole offseason when the Steelers didn't want to talk to me. Talk about God's perfect timing. I told my agent Brett the numbers, and he thought they were way too unrealistic. I said, "Brett, this is the contract." I admit that in the natural it was a big ask and probably unrealistic, but I had the Father negotiating for me. Brett did what I requested because he respected my corrections even when he didn't fully understand. We went to them with the numbers, and basically, the Steelers thought I was out of my mind. They threatened, "We can shut your whole career down by not only not negotiating but leaving you as you are." I said, "Brett, I would rather work a regular job nine to five on the principle of what I know the Holy Spirit showed me than negotiate down."

I said, "They can hold me hostage all they want." And they could. Remember, I was still fighting Reiter's syndrome, doing what I could with the bike and the swimming pool. Then, on Christa's third birthday, August 18, 1990, while we were at Chuck E. Cheese, I got a call from Brett. "You've got to go now. You're outta here. They traded you to the Washington Redskins for a player and a fourth-round draft choice." The Steelers got a player and a fourth-round trade, and they shipped me to DC. Boom, bam, I was gone. My head was spinning. The next day I went to John Cooke's office. He was the owner's son and president of the organization. Then, the prophetic dream came to the front and center of my mind. I was in the office, talking about my contract, and they gave me a three-year contract with the numbers. There may be a slight variation here or there, but they were basically the numbers I heard when God spoke to me in that dream through Todd's face. I signed that three-year contract with the Washington Redskins.

When I signed, I was still dealing with my physical issues.

They didn't just go away, so I signed the contract, along with a waiver. I got the numbers, good money now, but I had to sign a waiver that if I could not perform and the condition flared up, my contract would be voided and they would pay me nothing. I signed it and said, "What do I have to lose?" Every day, every single day, I was in pain. When I stepped on the field, however, grace hit me. It was incredible. I had enough grace to do my job well enough to make the team. I had gained some weight back, was a decent size, bulked up because I could lift weights again. Still, I would have to pack myself in ice to survive the next day.

In hindsight everything made sense, though it didn't when I was going through it. Before I collapsed, I was reading Psalm 73:26 one day, and it spoke to me—the Word spoke to me—and it said, "My flesh and my heart may fail, but God is the strength of my heart and my portion forever." I never realized that Bible verse was going to come alive in real time and be the anchor of hope for my whole life. I forgot that I had read that until months later. By the end of that season, I was healed. And the Holy Spirit said, "Do you know why you still love Me? Do you know why you didn't quit?" I would be in the hospital room praying, and it felt as if the ceiling were steel, that the Father had gone somewhere. The reason I didn't turn against Him, the reason I didn't quit is because He said, "My flesh…may fail," and my flesh had failed completely. I had no strength. It was him being the strength of my heart and my portion forever. There were days I would be in tears. I signed the waiver and played that season, and by the end of the season, I was healed.

TEMPTATION AT THE DOOR

When I first got traded from the Steelers to the Redskins, it happened so quickly. My family wasn't there, and I had to stay in a hotel in Virginia. When Christian friends from Penn

State started finding out I was there, they came to see me, and we got together at public places and fellowshipped along with some of the men of God on the team. They loved Jesus. We had young ladies in our senior class who were genuine friends. There was no shadiness, nothing immoral or anything. They were just good, solid friends. One particular young lady was friends with us guys, and was quite beautiful, but again, everything was on the up-and-up. We talked, and she was glad I was in town. I said, "Oh, great. Come over and see me." Now, I was in a hotel. She was in the hotel. It was the dumbest thing in the world I could have done. I was married with a child. I loved my wife, and I had a young lady in the hotel room with me. Yet in my naive mind I was cool. She was cool. We'd known each other for years. We had a great conversation, and there was nothing errant going on. All was well, and it came time for her to leave. She was going toward the door, and you know that real small space you stand at right before the door?

Something strange happened. It was as awkward as anything I had experienced up to that point. When she was about to walk out, a thought popped in my head: "Kiss her, get with her." The temptation of that wasn't there when we were talking, and she was the friend that she had been. When the temptation to sleep with her hit me that quickly, I got scared. I paused and took a deep breath, and my whole life flashed before me in that moment because one centimeter of a move in the wrong direction, and I hurt so many people and destroy every part of my life. Everything. I said, "OK" and let her out. I believe that touch of love that I encountered back at the table and the floor and the Father fathering me was the only reason I didn't fall to that temptation. I don't have any other explanation. The Father was showing me how to behave.

When I tell people I've been married for thirty-seven years and have never cheated on Le'Chelle, it doesn't mean I haven't been tempted. It just means I never gave in. And that's a miracle after playing ten years in the NFL and seeing guys have double, triple lives with other people in other cities and groupies and all of it. My life is absolutely a miracle. That temptation with my friend back in Virginia marked me to never do something that dumb again or assume. Let me state for the record, Le'Chelle and I had and have a wonderful relationship physically and emotionally. In the beginning she had felt the weight and pressure of the baby and the NFL life, but after that prophetic word she was set free, and our relationship went to a deeper level. I had no reason to desire another woman. I had no reason at all. I believe it was the whisper of the enemy: "If I can't take you down like this, I'm going to take you down." And not just take me down but the whole ministry, everything that God was doing. That pain that I caused my wife, I never wanted to cause again. I would rather die than hurt her like that again. I would rather be lifted from this earth than to go through that again.

It's worth noting here that five years into our marriage we were sitting in church as we normally did. Le'Chelle looked at me and said, "I trust you." Even though she had forgiven me when I first came clean before we were married, I had a long way to go to rebuild her trust. I went into the marriage saying, "I'm going to track myself. Everywhere I go, whomever I talk to will be available to my wife. To this day, Le'Chelle still has my password to my phone. I don't want any secrets. If she needs to know anything, she can ask. But in that five years, I had no room to give her any reason not to trust me. That wasn't because any man was telling me to do that. It was the Father showing me by His Spirit living in me, that taught me I didn't have a right to be angry, to be mad, to justify myself, to be the victim. It's because of what I did that we were there. Yet it's because of what Jesus is doing that will lead us out of here. I had to trust the Father's plan instead of my own for how to make things right. The more I trusted my heavenly Father, the more He showed my wife I could be trusted. This was a whole new way of life.

I grew up a completely different way, so it took a lot of learning and growing. I wasn't perfect, but my greatest reward was not only humbling myself, trusting Jesus to give me a new heart and a new spirit, a whole new way of living, but having my wife trust me. And there's nothing I was ever going to do to break that trust. So while I don't understand what my father went through in his brokenness, because I wasn't there, I now live with the hope of what it feels like to be healed by the truth from my own brokenness. Not the principles of truth but the person of truth, who is Jesus, and what it feels like to be a son because I have a heavenly Father. That now helps me to father my son and daughters. It was only through knowing the truth and pursuing this love that I began that journey and transition.

Love changes everything.

PRAYING FOR MY WIFE MAKES A DIFFERENCE

As our relationship grew, the Father was teaching me how to be the spiritual leader and do spiritual warfare for my wife and family. On one particular road trip, I walked into the hotel room as I had done many times before. All of a sudden, this burden to pray for Le'Chelle hit me. I started praying in tongues. I don't even know why, but for forty-five minutes, I was praying in tongues. Once I felt this sense of peace, and that grace to pray had lifted, I called home. Le'Chelle had driven down Route 28 and was in a three-car pileup. She walked away with not even a scratch. It was during the same exact time I was praying in tongues. The same exact time! If I don't understand what I'm praying for, I pray in the Spirit because the Spirit knows.

CHAPTER 12

SUPER BOWL LETDOWN

The cool thing is I played out my three-year contract with the Redskins, and it was incredible. I was honored to make the Sports Illustrated All-Pro Team and be voted the 1993 Redskin of the Year. We even won the Super Bowl! However, my greatest reward wasn't winning the Super Bowl, or the money. My greatest reward was the Father's presence in my life. I'm often asked to speak to business and community leaders and high-capacity people because I have been where they are or where they want to go. And that is at the highest level of the "game" of their lives—for me, the NFL All Pro and Super Bowl champion. Playing in the Super Bowl is one of those experiences that very few people ever get to have. Only about 3 percent of NFL players will ever dress out for the Super Bowl. And that's out of the less than 1 percent of players who actually make it to the NFL. As of the writing of this chapter there have been fifty-six Super Bowls—with a total of 5,936 players in history since 1967. That's out of the millions of people who would dream of that. The odds are beyond staggering. So to actually experience the game and then win the championship, that's against all odds. It's intoxicating.

Super Bowl week was like no other week in sports. Thousands of reporters. Media days. Interviews. Fans and family everywhere. Going through that week was mesmerizing. Joe Gibbs, however, put the hammer down on us for practice that week, which didn't make any sense to us. We had just won fourteen games. We went through everybody. And this is the preparation week, where you want to get guys to tighten up, get them ready. It was almost as if we went back to training camp. Guys were complaining. I think Joe Gibbs knew the complaints were his seal. He needed to make us markedly focused. We couldn't wait to get on that field. He was brilliant in preparing us. I would have thought to throttle back, dial practice down a little bit. But Super Bowl week carries a lot of distractions. You got family, friends, everybody wanting to come. Then there are activities. You can totally build up your whole season and lose it in a week if you don't discipline yourself and play it out the right way. It was quite an interesting experience.

The night before, they took us way outside of town in the middle of nowhere, down some remote roads to another hotel. We would have team meetings every now and again as players only if we needed them. Coach Gibbs wanted the players meetings to be us owning the team, not just from the coaches down. They had the vision, strategy, and accountability for us. I believe he wanted it to be us guys fighting for each other and really knowing how to play this game at a level where the vision can be something we *all* see.

Finally, on game day, we ran out of the tunnel, just as you've seen on TV growing up as a kid. The smoke. The lights. Hearing your name called. The roar. Oh my goodness, the feeling is indescribable. The whole world is watching this thing. The game was spectacular—the '91 Redskins were one of the best teams in Super Bowl history. Once it started, the game is the game, and it was back to football for us. We knew this was it. You win, or you lose and go home. We were playing against the Buffalo Bills, and it was back and forth. We won, and after the game it was mayhem. Confetti. Fans rushing the field. Reporters. The Vince Lombardi Trophy. Fred Stokes and I hoisted Joe Gibbs up, and it made the front page of the *Washington Times*. I was so excited, but it was draining after being on the field for so long.

I...THOUGHT, "OH MY GOODNESS, THERE'S A WHOLE WORLD OF PEOPLE WHO DON'T KNOW THE FATHER AND HAD EVERYTHING AND NOTHING AT THE SAME TIME."

For whatever reason, I got into the locker room earlier than the other guys. Maybe the Father arranged it to be that way, because the strangest thing happened when I exited the stadium, ran back through the tunnel, and stepped into the locker room. I had the most interesting, unexpected feeling I could have ever had. The emptiest, most hollow feeling I had ever felt in my life engulfed me. "Was that it?" It was over. The void and the sense of emptiness that I had heard about when I was first coming into faith—I felt it. What was paradoxical to me is I have a relationship with Jesus, so I'm not empty; there was a purpose to my life. I was preparing to leave. And right there in the locker room the Father *showed me that is what these other guys are feeling without Him*. It was supernatural. My compassion, my sense of "This is all they have," was amazing. That's why you see some of the greatest athletes who reached this height and had this experience become so intoxicated with it that they want that again. It's never enough. Most will never have it again. If they do, the euphoria lessens each time. I've looked at the players' faces and had divine insight into their souls, watched them win championships, and seen the law of diminishing return, seen the emptiness. I have seen it with my own eyes. I've felt it. I know what it looks like. But they keep retiring and unretiring, trying to get back to that place of doing to try to feel something and be something. I've had compassion and empathy for athletes who can't let it go, because I know what it felt like. For that moment, I felt empty. I felt everything I had worked all my life for was done. It was over, and I thought, "Was that it?"

I felt all that in the locker room and thought, "Oh my goodness, there's a whole world of people who don't know the Father and had everything and nothing at the same time." Sure, I celebrated like everybody else, but I never let it become who I am. As a result, I recovered extremely fast because I had the Father, who satisfied me.

Ironically, the night before at the remote hotel after the team meeting with the coaches, we had a players-only meeting where different guys got up to share about the game and what it would take to win it. I sat there and knew the Father had put a word on my heart, but it had nothing to do with the game. So after some guys spoke, I got up to speak. This is what I said: "We all have responsibilities that we have to take care of in life. We know the consequences if we don't. If we're not here, we won't experience certain things. We all ask those questions about what we're responsible for in life with family, kids, friends, and work, but do we ever ask God what He wants from us? He wants a relationship with us. There's something He wants us to do that's not just with this game; it's turning to Him to put our trust in Jesus to know how to live for Him after this game." Those aren't exact words, but that's what I put out there. It was interesting that in the midst of all that, the Holy Spirit nudged me and said, "Let's do something different." My burden was this game is going to be over. It was festive. It was dreamlike. Then these men will have to live their lives for something far greater lest they be lost.

CHAPTER 13

ONLY GOD AGAIN

After the Super Bowl, I finished my three-year contract with the Redskins. It was '93, and I was in full-blown negotiations again. All the while, my Reiter's syndrome was back with a vengeance. Similar to arthritis, it's inflammation in the joints from the neck down. And just as before, I couldn't train and do what needed to be done to play at that level. I knew this was going to be used against me in negotiations, which was totally understandable and fair. I wasn't trying to hide my condition, but I was most definitely trying to overcome it. The brutal fact is players in the NFL are investments, and if you can't continue producing and giving a solid return, you're out. It's just the nature of the business. I needed my body to work so my family could eat—and it was growing. In 1991 our second child, Kayla, was born, which only increased my capacity to love. I didn't know so much love was possible. Regardless of what I was going through, however, I was believing that the Father's will was going to be done. Period.

In March 1993 I went to another prophetic conference, this one in Houston, Texas, sponsored by Calvary Baptist Church. There were about twelve hundred in attendance, and it would once again prove to be the Father's divine guidance in having me there. The conference was led by Jack Deere and other powerful voices in the prophetic. What happened to me there and afterward was so supernatural the story made it into Jack

Deere's book *Surprised by the Voice of God*. Read Jack's own words:

> Tim Johnson was attending that meeting where I was speaking [with two others, unnamed]. At that time, Tim was an all-pro defensive lineman for the Washington Redskins. At the close of the 1992 NFL season, Tim thought God was leading him from the Redskins to another football team. But he wondered if it was really God speaking to him or might he just be reacting to some changes in his circumstances. By the spring of 1993, he was almost certain God was opening a door for a move to another team that would be professionally and financially rewarding. However, Tim had begun to have such excruciating pain in his back that he could no longer jog, let alone run. It developed to the point that it threatened to end his professional football career. [One of the speakers who moved in the prophetic] was introduced to Tim but was not told by him or anyone else about his injury or his planned move from the Redskins. One night after [he] finished speaking, he began to give prophetic words to people. He asked, "Where is Tim from the Washington Rednecks?" (This man was not one of your more knowledgeable sports enthusiasts.) Tim stood up. [The prophet] said, "Tim, you're in a place right now where promotion comes from the Lord. The Lord showed me in a very clear way that you have been in transition, and you are thinking about a move. The Lord showed me you are not going to make that move right now because he still has something wonderful for you where you are. The Lord is touching the back of your neck and your lower back. You don't look like you have that kind of trouble. You look like you're in the picture of health. But the Lord is going to heal that pain. Let's thank the Lord for this." That Easter Sunday, Tim woke

up and went to the park near his house. He began to jog and had no pain. Then he began to run. Still no pain. He was completely healed of his back and neck problems. Remember, [the prophetic word that was spoken over him] had said the Lord was going to do something wonderful for Tim in Washington, D.C.? He stayed with the Redskins for the 1993 season and had his best year in professional football. At the end of the season, he received a number of incredible awards. Among them, he was named the most valuable Redskin player by the Quarterback Club of Washington, D.C., an outstanding honor for a lineman. Had Tim left the Redskins, he would have missed a number of very rewarding things that happened to him.[1]

What Jack didn't tell you is the next day, I would be flying back to Virginia. Then, the pain was worse than when I went to the conference. I could barely make it through the airport. I was carrying bags, and I was screaming inside. If I would've dropped a bag, I would've fallen. For a couple of weeks leading up to Easter, the pain would be so intense I would have to pull off to the side of the road and just scream at the top of my lungs, "I'm healed. I know You healed me. I know it." And I would go out and try to run but couldn't do it. Go out and try to run. Couldn't do it. On Easter morning I just kept believing. I went out and took a step, then took another step, then jogged, and I was so out of shape. I came back home to Le'Chelle and said, "Honey, I'm so out of shape, but I can run. I can run!"

That ended up being my best season—103 tackles, 21 of them in one game against the Jets. I was named Sports Illustrated All Pro and MVP for the Redskins. The Father was fathering me!

DIVINE DETAILS AND FLEAS

I played another two years for the Washington Redskins, and at the end of the '95 season I signed with the Cincinnati Bengals as a free agent. They would turn out to be my last team, but I didn't know that '96 was going to be my last season. I trained for Camp in Virginia, which was now home to us. We'd built a life there, were living in a dream house, and had established relationships. We were settled in a wonderful church and were active in the community and schools. I wasn't looking to start over. By the way, our third child, Karrah, was born in 1995. She is another amazing experience of expanding my capability to love. Psalm 127:3 was ringing true: "Children are a heritage from the LORD, offspring a reward from him." So there were five of us now: Christa, nine years old; Kayla, five; Karrah, a year old; Le'Chelle; and me. This was my tenth year in the NFL. We would go to Cincinnati as a family and live in a nice apartment, and I would do my job for the season. Then, we'd come right back to our home in Virginia. That was the plan. When we first got to Cincinnati and moved into our apartment, another incident happened that showed through the divine details how much the Father cares not only for us but for the people around us. And it involved fleas. Yes, you read correctly, fleas.

We had gotten there and were all moved in, only to discover that fleas had infested our apartment to the point where Le'Chelle found fleas and Karrah's diaper. To top it off, exterminators couldn't get them out. So we had to hastily have a real estate agent find us a place that was furnished. We ended up in Blue Ash, a beautiful area just outside Cincinnati, in a spacious, fully furnished house in an incredibly nice neighborhood. All we needed to do was bring our clothes.

What I didn't realize was that the Father had a plan to

make Le'Chelle and me an access point for my teammates who were lost, along with their wives and girlfriends. By mid-season that house was packed with these teammates and others doing a Bible study. Our plan had been to go in, play the season, and get back home to Virginia. In and out, not getting deep into it because we were going back home to Virginia. However, the Father let me know that I was living a life in the NFL as His son. Therefore, I had to be available, and He put us in that home to make room for the souls He would bring for that Bible study. The apartment would've been too small. One of the young men in that Bible study was a quarterback on the team. Years later, in 2007, when we planted the church in Orlando, his sister started coming with her husband. Now they have two kids, and she's been one of our best leaders in the church. In Cincinnati we were sowing seeds for our future church in Orlando—all by opening up that house.

I went through the season, and we almost made the playoffs but came up short. The last part of the season, I suffered a slight tear in my rotator cuff, which is a hard injury to come back from. After surgery in the offseason, I labored to get to that elite level of training. I struggled but pushed to the best of my ability. I went back to camp for the next season, drove from Virginia to Ohio pulling a U-Haul. On the first day at camp they checked me out. I had trained and done everything to get to the elite level I was used to. It was a place I called "rare air." You have a lot of great athletes, but it's only when you go to that "rare" beyond-yourself level of training where it's elite. I knew what that felt like, and it was hard to get there. I'd had shoulder surgery and just couldn't get back there. Even so, I was a top player with a contract, so I went back to camp. When I had my physical, my shoulder didn't respond.

Later, I was heading out of the facility, and Tim Krumrie, the Bengals' defensive line legend, who had turned coach and was now coaching us, called me to go with him to the defensive line team meeting room. I could see he was physically nervous, and I said, "Tim, come on. I know how this works." He said, "Yeah, Mr. Brown wants to see you." He knew I knew what that meant. So I shook Tim's hand because it was so great being with him. We used to sit in the back of the meeting room like old friends, even though I only knew him personally for a little while.

After shaking his hand and thanking him, I went up to Mr. Brown's office. "Mr. Brown," I said, "I want to say thank you for this opportunity. I really appreciate all you have done for me." When thinking about retiring from the NFL, I often pondered the question "How will I know it's time?" Darrell Green, who was more than a friend and teammate—more like my brother—and I used to sit up late and talk about these things. He was a great man of God and probably the fastest man ever to play in the NFL. At one point he was the fastest man in the world. Darrell had an extensive and celebrated career, but we used to always have these conversations. We were roommates on the road.

One time I was lying on the floor, and we were dreaming about how to change the world. Art Monk, Charles Mann, Ernest Byner, and I developed The Good Samaritan Foundation, an organization where we would recruit young people and interview them about whatever profession they wanted to pursue past high school. We would find a person in that profession and match them with the inner-city student so the student could be exposed to that particular environment, mentored, and evaluated for the work they did in their summer internship. It broke the paradigm of these young people not believing there were any real opportunities in the world for whatever their interests, talents, and gifts were. It's heartbreaking to hear a kid you're interviewing about their goals in life say, "I just want to make twenty-one." He just wants to live to see twenty-one years old. There's no real foresight for what the future looks like, as far as flourishing in an occupation or gift. We would raise money for these kids to have those barriers broken by being in real environments with photographers, doctors, legislators, or lawyers. The paradigm also needed to be broken with the professional people, who may see inner-city kids as threats or throwaways. So we merged these worlds together. It didn't cost either one of them. We would pay the kids for a summer job because that's when crime rates are up and teenage pregnancy occurs, among other issues. We wanted to make sure they were preoccupied. Then, on Fridays, we would give them a cleanup or service project in their own neighborhood so they could be part of restoring their community, rather than always thinking their way out is to escape. If you can see what it looks like to go help Miss Jones down the street with her fence or cut her yard, for example, you begin to value where you're from. The answer isn't always to get out. It's to rebuild where you are.

We were so preoccupied with what we would do in the community that I didn't think a whole lot about what would happen afterward. One Thanksgiving we had around four hundred baskets of food. Art, Charles, and I had a big Hummer. It was such a fun day, driving up in the hood, bringing baskets of food, knocking on doors, and them being shocked at whom they saw. Back in those days the Redskins were like celebrities, with favor in the town. So to go into some of the worst places, knocking on doors, handing out food, just energized me.

WRAPPED IN PEACE

Back in Cincinnati, I left Mr. Brown's office and called Le'Chelle. "Honey, the Lord gave us ten years." She said, "What? You signed a ten-year contract?" I told her, "No, they cut me." She said, "Come on home." Driving back to Virginia and for the next three days, I could not shake the tangible presence of the Father's love. I felt His pleasure; I felt His delight in me. I felt saturated by His arms around me, basically saying, "I'm proud of you." You know those are the words that Jesus heard before He went into the wilderness to be tempted. "This is my beloved Son, with whom I am well pleased" (Matt. 3:17, ESV). There was nothing that Satan could offer Jesus to please Him. Yet when Satan offers us things, we are pleased with them because we don't know that we are the Father's son or daughter. When I began my career, the Father spoke to me and said, "Build a life in My son. Don't build a life in the NFL." And I knew what He meant. In whatever city I played for—Pittsburgh, Washington, DC, or Cincinnati—get planted in a church. Get taught as a disciple. Make disciples. Practice worship. Follow the Word. There were things that I knew in my heart were important to the responsibility of being an NFL football player, and I never disregarded them. But I always knew there was something greater about who I was called to be in it. Calling people back, showing up to places on time, not making excuses, being faithful—all these little things would demonstrate that I'm being raised differently. That three days were a deep affirmation and this time I didn't even ask for that. I just felt Him saying, "Well done. You did what I told you to do."

INSTEAD OF LETTING THE GAME, THE MONEY, AND GETTING INTOXICATED WITH THAT LIFESTYLE OF BEING IN THE BRIGHT LIGHTS CONTROL MY FUTURE, THE HOLY SPIRIT WAS TELLING ME WHO I WAS SUPPOSED TO BE.

I knew the Father had something He was moving me into that was out of the NFL. I called my agent and told him I was released and not to call me with another offer. I knew how this worked, how the game was played. Other teams always call, and if I would not have been secure in who I was, I would have been lost in that moment, looking for something else to do in the NFL. Sure enough, a couple of months later Le'Chelle and I were in Chicago at a friend's bar mitzvah, and I got the news from my agent that the Cowboys called offering me a contract. Now, at that time, I could have made half a million dollars, minimally, for the deal. Both Le'Chelle and I raised our eyebrows, but we knew the answer was no. Instead of letting the game, the money, and getting intoxicated with that lifestyle of being in the bright lights control my future, the Holy Spirit was telling me who I was supposed to be.

So I never entertained the Cowboys' offer. It's not that taking offers and playing the game is wrong, but for me it was time to let go because the Father had a new path He wanted to lead me on. When our identity is in Him and not our doing, we can make those transitions with peace. The Lord graciously blessed me with ten wonderful years in the NFL, a whole decade playing with three teams—the Pittsburgh Steelers, Washington Redskins, and Cincinnati Bengals. To cap it off, I was allowed the experience of playing in and winning the Super Bowl. And because the Father had walked with me through my career journey, when it was time to leave the game, I was ready.

CHAPTER 14

"YOU PARK HERE"

I was back in the Virginia-DC area settling into my new domestic life away from football. You have to understand that I had played every year since those Pop Warner days at Ringling Redskins Park, where coach Patella had lit a spark under me. For the past twenty-two of my thirty-three years, football had been in my life. At every level I have seen former NFL players go into deep depression and loss of identity when the game moved on from them. Yet here I was experiencing the peace that passes all understanding, which started when I drove home from Cincinnati and was continuing to envelop me.

When I began my journey in the NFL, the Father told me, "Prepare to leave. Build a life in My Son, not the NFL. I will Father you." That's how I journeyed through my entire professional football career, and He faithfully led me through, often in miraculous ways, as we've seen. Now, on this new leg of my journey, nothing had really changed except what I was *doing*. My identity was in Christ whether I was a defensive lineman in the NFL or a custodian in the locker room. Yes, I was in a season of transition as far as my *doing* was concerned, but my identity was the same. So were my instructions. "Build a life in My Son.... I will Father you." As I sought Him, listened to His voice and followed His Word, the Father would guide as always. I'm not talking about not having goals and dreams and ambitions. I'm not talking about not working harder than anybody else to be the best at what you do. I did that every time I trained or set foot onto the playing field or hit the books at Penn State. All that is important. We are each created with unique gifts that need discovering, developing, and pursuing. Finding your gifts and that distinct lane the Father has for you is where purpose comes, but not your identity.

Identity comes in a relationship with the Father through Jesus. Jesus said to Thomas, "I am the way, the truth, and the life. No one comes to the Father except through Me" (John 14:6, NKJV). Jesus is the way to the Father. Back in Genesis, Adam and Eve were given functions and assignments, but those things only brought wholeness when in the context of being in relationship with the Father. In other words, we can find purpose in our doing, but identity comes through intimate connection with the Father. When that relationship with His creation was fractured by sin, the Father loved us so much that He made a way for us to be reconciled back to Him through Jesus. "For God [the Father] so loved the world that He gave His only begotten Son" (John 3:16, NKJV). When we are not connected to our Father, the things we do, whatever they may be, will always fall short of ultimate fulfillment and often wind up enslaving us instead. However, when your identity is in the Father, you can have peace and fulfillment regardless of the season or place you're in, including those difficult ones. It's Colossians 3:23 again—"And whatever you do, do it heartily, as to the Lord and not to men" (NKJV)—except it's written on your heart, not only your taped wrist.

For the longest time there was a desire in me to be a lawyer. When in Cincinnati, I had contacted a professor at George Mason and asked him to mentor me and help prepare me for the LSAT. Education had always been a priority, so studying hard was never an issue. As I learned more about the justice system, knowing that it's the hinge on the door that locks people out and lets people into the mainstream, I wanted to go where the game was played. My cousin was a successful lawyer in Atlanta with integrity whom I really looked up to. It's a noble profession and what I thought I wanted to do. This seemed to be the direction I was headed in, but I wasn't totally focused on it.

I was also looking into some business opportunities. Ministry opportunities seemed to always be there, mainly in the form of speaking. I had written a three- and a five-year plan, which included an inner-city ministry that I wanted to do. There was actually a ministry that a friend exposed me to that was doing everything I wrote in a ministry vision for the inner city. It was called Frontline Outreach. My friend was helping them search for an executive director to fill a vacant role, so I flew down to Orlando to do an interview. Everything I saw being done regarding ministry at this nonprofit organization was very much in my heart. My friend worked for Prison Fellowship at the time. He knew some of the board members who were doing an executive search, and he recommended me. In the process I was thinking, "OK, I've got a mentor for the LSAT for Law School. I'm traveling. I'm in eldership training in my church. I'm looking at possibly starting a business, but I also want to make a difference in the work that's going on in inner cities." There was a lot going on inside my mind, and as you can see, I had several options. It was impossible for me to do all these things, and I couldn't do one until the Father opened my eyes to see His plan. Fortunately, the NFL had been good to me, so financial pressure wasn't an issue, which was a blessing. Still, I had to figure out what to do with the rest of my life.

The Lord had led us to Grace Covenant Church, a wonderful and strong fellowship that was now family. I was giving financially and was part of the prayer team and discipleship and children's ministry. We were involved, doing lots of things. I had even gotten involved in eldership training. The Lord was showing up in the training sessions, stretching us, growing us. One day I pulled up in the church parking lot, and similar to when the Holy Spirit spoke to me in the locker room to "clean it up," He said, "You park here. You don't live here."

I was thinking, "But I've been faithful, Lord."

But it was my heart. Despite participating in the eldership training, I was caught up in all the career options I had and was pretty distracted from giving my heart fully to the church. I wasn't all there. Actually, I'd been pulling back, not pulling back from the Father but from the church. I'll tell you one important reason. You need to know. One of the pastors who had been a spiritual father to me early on back in Penn State had experienced a quite public moral failure. I was devastated. It hit me hard. I just cried. He ended up having an affair with an employee's wife. There are no words to describe the devastation. There are people today who still haven't recovered from that. I was in the fetal position, grieving and in tears, after I heard what had happened to him. I had looked at this man in reverence and idolized him, not in a weird way but would do anything for him. He was one of my pastors. He was my spiritual father because he was so gracious. Under him I grew and got a sense of purpose. After his fall I cried like a baby. It hurt so deep. I felt a little bit lost after that, thinking, "What am I going to do now? Where do I go?" I was on the ground, bawling, and this scripture in Deuteronomy came to mind. It talked about when the plagues hit Israel and people were dying off. But those who clung to the Lord had stayed alive. So the Father just whispered that encouragement to my heart, and that became my answer. I decided, "I'm clinging to You, Lord, so I don't die, I don't drift, I don't wither spiritually." The situation hurt me deeply, but that word became healing to me. Yet I found myself still becoming leery of trusting leadership.

In addition, at another church I was involved with in Pittsburgh, the pastor was caught in disguise renting pornographic videos from the video store. In that situation, I was part of having to confront him. Look, I'm just being real here. I think what happened to me was I told myself, "OK, I don't need you guys. I'll do this walk myself." Leadership failure is one of those things the enemy loves exploiting in order to discourage both believers and nonbelievers from church. It also gives ammunition to the antagonists. The truth is, we should never put our complete trust in any man. All of us are flawed. From time to time we've all been failures in some form or fashion in desperate need of God's grace washing us and picking us back up. While it's true that because leaders have such responsibility and are in the public eye, they are held to a higher standard, the Father is still always about the healing and restoration. Often the restored leader becomes more effective. Nonetheless, my trust had been broken, and I'd been pulling up to church but had not completely trusted.

Sometimes, though, the gate of trust that's broken is the gate He brings us back through. I never would have said this at that time, but I had been through some craziness. What's interesting is before all that happened, I had received a prophetic word from prophet Bob Jones that Le'Chelle and I would learn what to do and what not to do over the many years in ministry. That was definitely playing out. So when I pulled into the parking lot and the Father said, "You park here," it was a bit disruptive to what I believed the Father wanted me to do. I was doing all this good stuff. I was doing what I knew to do. I was doing what I thought were the right things. I had godly ambition. Yet the truth is, it's great to be faithful, but to be rooted is different.

My pastor at Grace Covenant, Brett Fuller, I still consider my pastor today. He was also the chaplain for the Howard University Bisons. I had met Pastor Brett in training camp the year before I got traded. For more than thirty-two years we've maintained a close relationship. He has been a spiritual father to me. Like all of us, he is not a perfect man, but he is one of the most honorable men I know. That said, when I pulled into the church parking lot that morning, though I was involved, my heart was divided, and I was serving from a distance. The Holy Spirit wanted more, not because He wanted me to work more but because He wanted me to *become* more. Like the times before, the voice was unmistakably His. After leaving the church, I went home and told Le'Chelle, "I had this moment right in front of the church. I need to do something, and I need you to come with me. I have to go to Pastor Brett's house and submit my life to him completely." My wife is no pushover, and she's not flaky. This had to be the Holy Spirit showing me this. She's not hyper-spiritual but is very pragmatic, wise, sensitive to the Spirit of God. Le'Chelle went along with it. So we got Christa, Kayla, and Karrah, and all of us went to Pastor Brett's house. I explained to him what I felt. I said, "Pastor Brett, I'm submitting my life to you to be under your authority. Tell me what to do. Just don't mess up my life." There was a soberness because I had heard what the Father had said. I submitted my life to Him, and all those great ideas that I had started to dissipate. I went from traveling and doing all those different things to being in a discipleship course. I was teaching, and the group went from around five people to three people. I was shrinking it. I thought, "Something's wrong here." I was looking for ministry success, and the Father was teaching humility and to trust in Him in the ministry. It was the Father humbling me to say, "It's me. I want you to know how I want to do this." I remember reading in John 3:30, "He must increase, but I must decrease," and I felt that was one of the scriptures that marked me. I must decrease; He must increase. All the things I had going, with different ministries and more, I put to the side. When I surrendered to the Holy Spirit's instruction and parked myself under Pastor Brett, my own plans got realigned with the Father's, which would ulti-mately prove to be what my heart and soul wanted all along. I just didn't know it. It's amazing how the Father does that. He knows us and loves us more than we do ourselves. So I put my agenda on the shelf, submitted to Pastor Brett, and just started serving up close.

It wasn't a year later that Rice Broocks, then the president of Every Nation and a pastor in Brentwood, Tennessee, just outside Nashville, came to our church as an apostolic leader to minster to us who were becoming elders. He wrote the *God's Not Dead* books, on which the movie *God's Not Dead* was based. As he was laying hands on us and praying, when he got to me, he stepped back with tears in his eyes. Later, Rice asked Pastor Brett what he was going to do with me. Long story short, Pastor Rice asked me to walk alongside him in leading the church in Brentwood. We submitted the idea to the Father and took time to pray about it. For Le'Chelle and me to uproot our family, it would have to be a Word from the Holy Spirit to both our hearts that we knew was unquestionably from Him. It took a little while for us to come to that point. Le'Chelle didn't agree right away, just because there were so many prac-tical, moving parts to our lives and we were really settled in our house in Ashburn, Virginia. One of the biggest fights we ever had was when we were considering the move to Nashville. She was dropping me off at the airport. A little while after that I started going back and forth to Nashville to minister. This became the first step in the transition to Nashville to become a pastor for the first time in a city I would never have chosen.

I don't even know what the big blowup was about, but it was so intense that I said, "I'm not getting out of the car. If I'm not supposed to do this, I'm not going to do this. I'll turn this away. I'll reject this. I'm not going to do it until we are right. We have to be right." I didn't want my integrity to be in question because of always doing things out of the box and my family's left behind. We got through that moment and ultimately got the release to go, which included the Father's enveloping peace in both of our hearts. Pastor Brett gave us the charge. "This is how you go. You go serve." The word was to go and serve Pastor Rice in whatever way he needed serving as unto the Lord. Be faithful and let everything else be put to the side of focus. We didn't know it going in, but the Lord was setting us up for the role of being a reconciler in a divided city. We moved in March 2000, and for the next seven years Brentwood and the Nashville area would be our home, where we saw unparalleled reconciliation.

It was also summer 2000 that our fourth child, a son, was born. His name is Shaun. When Shaun was born, he had four mothers and one dad. But that was a humbling experience for me because again, back when I was a kid, one of the things I was always aware of was to not be too needy. I wanted to be more dependent on what I could do. I wanted to be low maintenance, even in my relationship with the Father, to not put a demand on that. So it was very humbling to realize *we were going to have a son*. It was beautiful and powerful. *Humbling* is the word that comes to my mind the strongest because I didn't think I deserved to have a son. I don't know why, maybe because I didn't necessarily expect to have a son or know what to do with one. Coaching, mentoring, and helping young men and kids is different when it's your blood. Everything was completely new with Shaun. Over the years to come, as the

Father fathered me, He would teach me to father my son and be a comma, not a period, leading Him to the Father.

MAKING HISTORY

At that time, if you were traveling into Brentwood on I-65, it'd be almost impossible to miss the imposing statue and shrine of Confederate Lt. Gen. Nathan Bedford Forrest. He's waving a pistol in the air while riding a stallion that's reared up on its back legs flanked by a half-moon of about a dozen Confederate battle flags. Nathan Bedford Forrest was the founder of the Ku Klux Klan. Because the monument was private property, they could display it in public. This was the spirit we were up against. Of course, Nashville is Music City, home of the Grand Ole Opry and countless recording studios, record labels, publishing houses, and entertainment headquarters, and is one of the country's most happening hubs of activity. A beautiful place, Brentwood is home to many country music legends and entertainment moguls and CEOs and is one of the wealthiest and fastest-growing communities in the nation. It is also predominantly white.

Now I'm coming in. Because Pastor Rice was a man of deep courage, he believed that the kingdom of God should be ethnically diverse and reconciled. I had gotten the word to go and stand with him in the midst of this. We did a huge billboard/banner campaign that started above the Nathan Bedford Forrest shrine. The banner had a black hand and a white hand joined together and the seven locations around Nashville with "Bethel World Outreach Center reaching a city to touch the world." That became a banner of reconciliation and unity. It changed the spiritual climate in the city, I felt, because the church grew from eight hundred to almost three thousand by 2005, a three-year period. The sign was reaching a city that touched the world. There was other advertising on radio and television, and most of all, Pastor Rice was a powerful evangelist, and the Holy Spirit was present in the meetings. People from diverse backgrounds would come and leave empowered, encouraged, and moved by an overwhelming spirit of love. One time a Muslim lady cried the whole service. She said she had never seen anything like this before. The love was contagious and spread through the city. Something else powerful and cool is there used to be a regulation in Tennessee that no person of African descent or blood could own the property at Granny White and Old Hickory, the location of Bethel World Outreach. In 2005 they laid hands on me to become the first black senior pastor of a congregation of which the majority was white on what used to be a slave plantation. That was monumental. It was historic. The reconciliation ran deep.

Bethel was a pretty happening place when we were there, and still is today. Musicians would come to listen to the music, then Pastor Rice would preach, and I would exhort. It just was a very animated, dynamic environment. The presence of God was real. People loved the whole experience. So just like any other Sunday, you don't know who you would see in Bethel. In those seven years I was humbled and honored to pastor many famous people who attended our church and some who were outside our church. I had a life group with businessmen and athletes with various levels of influence.

The Lord allowed both Le'Chelle and me to minister to many spiritually orphaned musicians. Whitney Houston, whom we met through CeCe Winans, was one. Behind the scenes we began to have conversations with her and speak into her life without needing anything or wanting anything. We just loved her for who she was. She was made in the image of God but had been through a lot. We used to talk on the phone at least once a week. We took part in an intervention with her and

Bobby Brown. Le'Chelle and I had a moment to pray for them, pray with them, and be an encouragement to Whitney.

Once, while I was with DC Talk and had been traveling with TobyMac, we were going to Pulaski, Tennessee, for one of their concerts. We were pulling into town on the tour bus, and someone said, "Look out the window." We looked, and a KKK rally was walking right beside our bus. They were dressed in hoods and white sheets, the whole works. We were stunned, in disbelief. We went to the venue that was located right outside the town hall square. Michael Tait, the Black member of DC Talk, and I walked up there with Kevin Max and TobyMac. We were the only two Blacks up there. We went to the KKK rally and were across the street. The little town hall was right in front of us. Then there was a street, and then some little shops. We just stood there in disbelief. This is the 2000s, and this is where we still are? The concert went great, and they were a picture of reconciliation as well. Sometimes in order to overcome a culture, you have to have the opposite spirit of the culture. That's how we approached it. We were operating in the opposite spirit.

THE LORD ALLOWED BOTH LE'CHELLE AND ME TO MINISTER TO MANY ORPHANED MUSICIANS. WHITNEY HOUSTON, WHOM WE MET THROUGH CECE WINANS, WAS ONE.

The Holy Spirit was calling us to Nashville to be reconcilers, doing this incredible White man, Black man work. I'm the senior pastor, and the church is three thousand and continuing to explode. The Spirit of the Lord was moving powerfully. We had started new congregations in Clarksville and Murfreesboro and begun a major multimillion-dollar campaign for expansion on the Granny White/Old Hickory property in Brentwood. Then, we were going to build a con-gregation in Franklin. While it was going to be a lot of money, we got the plans together and worked out the details, and I was right in the center of it, while Rice Broocks was the bishop over all the congregations.

CHAPTER 15

OUT OF NOWHERE

While playing in the NFL our family would often go on vacation with some of my teammates and their families. It was fun that way, and Orlando, Florida, was one of our favorite destinations because of all the attractions and resorts. But other than a great vacation spot, it was simply another city. We didn't have any family or friends who lived there, no connections. I had no aspirations to live in Orlando. It was 2006, and I'd been the senior pastor in Brentwood for about a year. To get some much-needed R & R, our family took a vacation to Orlando again. Once there, we were having our usual great time, nothing out of the ordinary—we'd done this a hundred times.

One morning I decided to go play a round of golf and headed down State Road 417, looking forward to a peaceful few hours on the green. I was driving along, just chilling, when out of nowhere there came a visitation in the car. The Holy Spirit filled the vehicle with His presence, and I was driving down the street in tears. It was the table, the floor, all over again. I couldn't stop crying, and I was hearing, feeling an impression that I was to come plant a church in Orlando. This was not in my mind. I didn't even know what to do. I continued on and played golf. After that I came back and told Le'Chelle, and she didn't really even have words. She was not responding. I understood. What do you do with something like that? I mean, everything was going well in Nashville. My answer was yes, but I felt as if I should maybe just sit on this, because I didn't know what else to do. In my view the timing couldn't be more wrong. We were having such success in Brentwood. The Father was blessing. His favor was on us. Not to mention we were in the middle of this multimillion-dollar campaign. How do you tell the then bishop of the city churches, the regional churches, and announce to the people, "Oh, by the way, I'm leaving." I was the pastoral presence on the ground over many, many people.

After vacation we went back to Nashville, and I didn't say a word, but like a nagging pebble in my shoe, that Holy Spirit word never left me. It was always right below the surface, and I kept it pushed down there for a while. Slowly, though, I began exhibiting some odd physical issues such as lethargy and depression, which was not my character at all, not even my makeup. I didn't understand it. Something was off. I felt out of alignment. Finally, I convinced myself to go see a doctor. After he took one look at me, he said, "What's wrong with you?" I thought, "Ain't it your job to tell me?" Instantly, it came to me. I knew. I've got to share the word with the leadership and do what I was being instructed to do. I didn't realize that holding on to a word that I was supposed to share strategically and not just in mass was breaking my body down. Not responding because I didn't know what to do with it was physiologically affecting me. I told Le'Chelle, "We've got to go see Pastor Rice."

We lived in the same neighborhood, maybe one or two minutes away, yet that drive could have been two weeks. It was the longest drive in the history of driving, going down the hill, around the corner, and having to share with him the word that I got. It was not easy, because so much was at stake. There was so much we were seeing happening, things that we planned to do as a church. Along the way I learned that when people respond to news or ideas differently than we expect, it's because they often don't understand. They're processing the best they know how. I realized I had to be careful how I presented myself, particularly this Orlando word, because every seed that I was sowing then was going to be sown into my future. For Pastor Rice, it was a scratch-the-head moment like, "Why now?" He was close to saying, "That's not God," and wanted to figure out how to keep me there. How do we make this work? And not just Pastor Rice but other leaders were asking the hard questions, trying to figure out why and how and not understanding. I can't say that I understood everything either. One thing Pastor Rice did understand was if something is from God, we shouldn't go against it but facilitate it. That's ultimately what happened. Bethel would come beside us in the effort.

Le'Chelle was steady because of all we had been through. She wasn't against it because the move from Virginia had prepared her for whatever was next. That's where she was most rooted. In Pittsburgh we were trying to figure out life. Virginia was where we found family and put down our roots. We had a great pastor who ministered to us, taught us, and fathered us well. There was no reason in the natural for us to leave Virginia, but I think the Holy Spirit extracting her out of there gave her more of a freedom to say yes to whatever He was saying. She was sturdy.

We were having dinner one night with Donna Summer and her husband. Donna moved in the prophetic and said surprisingly, "I see you guys going south." I was like, "Yeah, yeah, we're going to plant a congregation in Franklin one day." Franklin was south of Brentwood. She said, "No, no, no, further south." Le'Chelle and I looked at each other as if thinking, "She doesn't even know what she's saying." At that point, we weren't at liberty by the Spirit or our leaders to say anything to anyone. This was very tight, close to the vest, because I was a central figure in the campaign and the stability of the church. I was the boots-on-the-ground pastor. Pastor Rice is an apostle. He was traveling the world. He's truly a pioneer. When I became the senior pastor, it gave him the freedom to actually do that. I was the last person he wanted to see leave, and I had no plans of my own to leave. Yet it wasn't up to me. The Holy Spirit had His own plans, and we had learned to trust that His ways are always higher than ours, even when we don't understand the why or how. It took a whole year and a half to transition through all the emotions, all the questions, all the possibilities, and as it had been when leaving Virginia, we ended up being sent with blessings and the church supporting us.

THE HOLY SPIRIT HAD HIS OWN PLANS, AND WE HAD LEARNED TO TRUST THAT HIS WAYS ARE ALWAYS HIGHER THAN OURS, EVEN WHEN WE DON'T UNDERSTAND THE WHY OR HOW.

In January 2007, once the church in Nashville knew we were called to Orlando, that it was the Lord's doing, we assembled a prayer/transitioning team. We started praying twice a month in Nashville and traveling to Orlando twice a month, doing Bible studies and laying foundations, until we moved that July. Pastor Rice was still there, and Pastor James, one of the men I had mentored and discipled, stepped up in my place. In the Father's perfect timing it was a good transition for us from Nashville. We moved to Orlando on July 7, 2007, and our storage space was 2007.

Because we had to sell our Nashville house in the middle of a pretty bad market, we didn't have a house yet. This is when the market started to go down for housing. In fact, we would still be in Nashville if someone from Arizona hadn't bought our house for cash. Did I say for cash? That rarely happens, and our house wasn't cheap. We lived in a very nice neighborhood. It was another provision from the Father at the perfect time. We continued the Bible study through the summer, and in fall 2007 we did our first preview service.

BE A GOOD FINDER; EXPECT A MIRACLE

Before we moved to Orlando, I went down on a scouting trip and met with a pastor in the nearby Lake Nona area who was part of a church-planting network. He knew the history of the area well. His opening words to me were, "Yeah, over the last ten years there've been three hundred church plants here, and none of them survived." I thought, "Great, that's encouraging." When we got to Orlando permanently, we continued with the Bible studies throughout that summer. After three months, in October 2007, we started our preview services. Preview services typically consist of your launch team and a few others. Our launch team was a little unique, however. Back in Nashville when I announced we were planting a church in Orlando, people thought I was not thinking straight. They were sure of it when they found out my strategy: Plant with a full staff before having any members. In the natural that seemed backward. Who does that, right? But we were following the Holy Spirit's leadership and were used to trusting His out-of-the-box methods. Out-of-the-box doesn't mean being foolish, though. It requires prayer and listening and walking in the Spirit. One of the gifts of the Spirit is wisdom. Often the Holy Spirit gives divine wisdom that goes against our ordinary way of thinking, for extraordinary results. The Spirit told us to lay a solid foundation before anything else, and the Father would send the wounded souls. That's what the Father does. Jesus said, "No one can come to Me unless the

Father who sent Me draws him" (John 6:44, NKJV). We do as we are instructed, and the Father does the drawing. He did, and we were ready.

Born and raised in Manila, Philippines, Joel and Jenny Magpantay, who had never lived outside the Philippines, were our children's pastors. I can still remember them coming down the escalator in the Orlando airport at 6 a.m. to meet me. It was their first time living in the States. However, planting The Orlando World Outreach Center was a massive step of faith for everyone involved, not just Le'Chelle and me, or the Magpantays. Reaching Orlando and then the world was our vision, but we had to reach across the street first. You start there and build up little by little doing targeted evangelism and some minimal advertising. You build up to the big launch, where you pull out all the stops.

During this preview stage we worked through many of the kinks. Getting from point A to points B through Z was going to take significant time and provision, supernatural provision. I had a full-time staff that had to be paid, and we didn't have official members. We did the preview services until January of 2008 when we had our big grand opening service. Three hundred people showed up, which was phenomenal, and people came in from out of town. More importantly, Jesus showed up! CeCe sang, ushering in the presence of God in a powerful way. We were in a wonderful facility too, which I have to tell you about. It was one of the many miracles of provision.

The reason I'm telling you this whole story is to let you know the Father wants to guide you too in every aspect of your life. Building a church from scratch with the Holy Spirit's instruction is no different from building a marriage, or letting Him walk you through your personal experiences, building a life His way, in His Son. Since the Father had said, "I will Father you," my whole life has centered around listening for

His voice, using discernment, and following His lead, even when doing so seemed radical. He's never failed me.

On our visits to Orlando before the move, we had come to town because we had many questions and needed answers. "Where are our kids going to go to school? Where are we going to meet? What's the city like?" We had done demographic studies and researched all the different aspects of the city, such as its population, from a distance, but we needed to be on the ground. One of our first priorities was finding a good school for our kids. We had heard about a school called Lake Highland. Le'Chelle and I got directions to go there, but we ended up going in the wrong entrance to the parking lot, the side entrance. When I got out of the car, I immediately noticed a huge banner on the side of the building that said "Expect a Miracle." I went around to the other side of the car and opened the door for Le'Chelle. "Look at this sign," I said. "This is discouraging because we need a lot of those. We need a lot of miracles." I wasn't encouraged, because I was thinking, "I'm way out here now. I'm out here, moving my family, turning away a huge congregation, growing all this stuff, and feeling like I'm landing on nothing."

That day, however, the miracles started. We went in and met with the principle of the middle school campus we were on; he was a nice, sports-minded guy. We hit it off. Our whole focus was our kids going to school. As we were leaving, he asked, "What are you guys moving to Orlando for?"

"We moved here to plant a church," we said.

"Oh," he said. "What kind of church?"

"A diverse one," I said.

"Well, if you want to do that, this is the perfect location." I was thinking he meant the building, but later I found out he was talking about Orlando because Orlando is diverse. I took what I thought he was saying, followed up on it, and asked if we could meet in that building. I don't know if he was surprised or shocked, but he just adjusted to it.

We desperately needed a place to even know how to start this thing. Eventually, we negotiated starting the church in that building, and that sign on the side of the building started years of miracles. It started that day—for the first five years they charged us nothing to meet there. We had to set up and break down, but it had everything we needed. Did I mention they charged us *nothing*? How often does that happen?

The banner read "Expect a Miracle" on one side and "Be a Good Finder" on the other. It was the theme of the school and "Be a Good Finder; Expect a Miracle" became a theme of our church for years, seeing the favor of God. We ended up staying there ten years, and after the first five years they only charged us fifteen hundred dollars a month because they had to charge us something. It was a wonder-filled favor, and a lot of great things happened in that building. In appreciation our church would serve the school in any way we could. We even had people who eventually got hired as teachers or in administrative roles. We had a great relationship.

In the beginning when I shared with a few people the vision of starting the church in Orlando and of what we were believing for, a neighbor in Nashville gave us a substantial gift. Also, Bethel supported us significantly, at least to cover my family and me. The rest had to be by faith. I remember sitting in my office after the first year just overwhelmed. Le'Chelle came in and I was staring off into the distance. "What's wrong with you?" she asked. I didn't have an answer. She said, "Wait, wait, wait, you can't do this to me. I need you to give some answers." I realized I didn't have the resources to maintain what we had, the staff and everything else. I didn't have the resources. I rarely get overwhelmed, so I'm not even going to say I was stressed. It felt more as if I were dying, as though the air were being sucked out of me. There was no stress. I was just sitting there feeling like I was dying. The pressure was so great, and all I knew was to trust the Father because I had no other answer. We were either going to survive, or we were going to die.

I was sitting there feeling as though I was at the threshold of a near-death experience, and the Father came through. Let me tell you. He came through because if He didn't come through, we were through. That's a fact. We were done. The Father provided the resources we needed. Without going into detail too much, I was able to sell a piece of land that I had for my family. It enabled us to get through that season. When I tell people we gave all we had, we did it. The church started to grow as people were getting saved, baptized, and set free. That's what it's all about. It's not about me but about allowing myself to be a conduit for the Father to flow through. That doesn't mean the enemy hasn't tried to stop that flow, though.

WOMAN AT THE ALTAR

The altar is an interesting place. We've seen the Father meet people there and minister to them there. I remember one time a lady came up to the altar looking very unassuming—she wasn't in any way peculiar; she looked like a normal, average person. She seemed to be put together and cordial. She was standing there, and somehow we were in a conversation and she said, very mildly and plainly, that this ministry was going to go down, that this ministry was not going to make it, and some other crazy stuff. At first, it caught me off guard because I just couldn't believe I was hearing this. She seemed like such a nice lady. But she said it. I had to collect myself. I was thinking, "Hang on a second. This is not the Lord speaking. This is dark. This is the devil speaking." So I was very polite and simply said, "I don't receive that. That's not the God I know. My Father loves me. He loves His people. He will bless us." Then I excused myself. A lot happens down there at the altar, enough to write a book about just that.

How Can We Serve?

The city of Orlando was participating in a churchwide campaign called "Do Something." Realizing this was an opportunity for our congregation to serve our community, I went to the mayor's office and met with his chief of staff and some of his administrative team. I was new in town. They didn't know me from a man on the moon, and I said, "How can we serve the mayor? We have thirteen thousand hours to offer of service. We have a small congregation. We just want to participate in the well-being of our city."

One of the administrators responded, "I've been here in this city twenty years, and no pastor has ever come and said, 'I want to give you something.'"

"We want to be good neighbors," I said. "I'm not here to ask for anything." That was one of the things that set the tone for who we were going to be in seeking the well-being of our city. Our vision statement is "to be a community of disciples, discipling communities for Christ." There is no discipleship without relationship. We wanted to be good neighbors. We wanted to be an asset, not a liability. We wanted to be a blessing, not a burden.

We ended up helping the mayor start a reading program. We also had two hundred–plus people do a big cleanup project in a park with the mayor. We painted a shelter for those who suffered domestic violence, did landscaping, and went around neighborhoods picking up trash, needles, and all kinds of paraphernalia. One of those years, we walked around Amway Arena doing a neighborhood cleanup the day before the NBA All-Star Game was coming to town. We constantly found ways to serve in the city. We wanted to be clear that we didn't have any motives other than serving. We didn't have some religious agenda to create separation between church and state. We wanted to serve. I have such a passion and desire to mobilize people to participate in making an impact in the different events or activities we've done. One year I asked some of my NFL buddies to come to town, and we did a free football clinic at the stadium. That attitude was contagious at our church and grew into a lot of other impactful things.

Since our congregation has started meeting, we consistently ask ourselves, "Is faith alive?" It's not just some religious, trite thing. Just as Jesus said, "When the Son of Man comes back, is He going to find faith?" It's not preaching, music, gifts, all those things. Faith in Christ is my life. If there is a desire to have certainty in the midst of uncertainty, the gap between the two is called faith. That's where faith lives. If my faith is alive, it brings life everywhere I go. That's the subtle message we are trying to communicate.

CHAPTER 16

GOLF COURSE WORD

One day in December 2012 I went out to play golf. I was walking on the golf course and didn't remember what hole I was at, but I felt a deep impression from the Holy Spirit. It felt almost audible, to the point where I looked around to see if anybody was there with me, though I knew I was alone. The impression was so heavy and profound, with pictures flashing through my mind of me walking across the state and praying. Somehow I clearly understood that to mean "Walk across the state of Florida and pray." There was no mistaking it. Now I was overwhelmed, walking on the golf course, looking around like, "Does anybody hear this?" It was so extraordinary that I didn't know what to do with it. Sidenote: I either need to stop playing golf, or I need to play a lot more golf. I lined up to hit my ball, and it was the best golf shot I'd had all day. I was just in another zone. If every shot were as seamless as that one, I'd be on the PGA Tour. It was like the voice freed me up.

When I finished with the round, I was shaking inside, trying to process everything. "Where do I go with this?" My family and I happened to be having lunch together that afternoon. I was holding all this in but about to burst. I'm always looking for the witness of what the Father is saying to me from Le'Chelle because she's so discerning and wise. She helps keep me from getting off track. She doesn't necessarily understand

151

every impression, vision, or idea I share with her, but she knows whether something is from the Father's heart. My plan was to wait and tell Le'Chelle when we were alone, but as I sat there at lunch, I thought "They can call me crazy, but I'm just going to spill it out." My kids were practically grown at this point, and everybody was there, so it felt like a divine setup. So as we were sitting there, I said, "I have some news to share. I just had the most interesting, amazing experience. I don't really know if this is the Lord, but I believe He's telling me to walk across the state of Florida and pray." I shared it all.

I was waiting for somebody to burst out, "That's the stupidest thing I've ever heard! You're out of your mind!" I was sitting there, waiting for the words, calm but bracing myself. It was one of those things you don't hear every day. At some point, I can't remember who, but one of my kids said, "That's a great idea, Dad!" I was thinking, "It is? Seriously? Are you serious?" And then they started trying to plan it. "We can do this!" I thought, "What is happening right now?" Le'Chelle slowly entered the conversation and tossed in a few planning ideas, not with deep conviction, though. It was a subtle cosign.

After that I walked through it with my leaders, a couple of my mentors, and everybody was taken aback by it. It seemed extreme. I said, "If anyone doesn't agree or has a different word from the Father, please tell me, and I won't do it." I was looking for people to tell me no. I was practically asking them to tell me, "No, don't do this." I said, "If you hear differently, I'll submit." They were concerned. There was hesitation, but no one could tell me no. Therefore, I said yes. It seems to be a pattern in my life—the Holy Spirit speaking to me to do out-of-the-ordinary things and me saying yes.

About a month later, in January, I decided I would do this. It was going to be a long 698 miles from Pensacola to South Beach, so I might as well get started. With that I put on a pair of shoes and socks and began walking. Of course, I did everything wrong. At the time, my home was in Baldwin Park, and I had a route planned. I can't remember all the streets, but I made it a mile or so, and my feet were killing me! I had the wrong shoes and socks and already had a blister on my foot. I called one of my kids and said, "You've got to bring me some shoes." The next day, I don't know how, but I ended up walking about ten miles. I muscled through it, knowing I had to do this. The morning after the ten-mile walk, it felt as if I'd been hit by an 18-wheeler. I could hardly move. I was thinking, "What in the world did I sign up for?" But I knew I couldn't stop, that the Father had spoken to me by the Holy Spirit to use this walk to glorify Jesus. Somehow it had to happen.

I remembered a friend of mine, Jimmy Wayne, who's an award-winning country music artist. In 2010 he walked halfway across America (from Nashville to Phoenix) to raise awareness for kids aging out of the foster care system. I called him up and asked, "Hey, man, what did you do? What was your strategy? Where'd you sleep? What was your footwear? What about the weather and safety?" He began to tell me about shoes and liner socks and all these other things. I had to get educated quickly on what this was going to look like for me. I got the best walking shoes, liner socks, all the proper equipment, and started training. Eventually I could walk ten to twelve miles from Baldwin Park to Casselberry and back. I got to where I could do that a couple of times and would do that three or four times a week. Then I would walk seventeen miles from Baldwin Park to Avalon Park. From January to March, I clocked about three hundred miles to get in condition and make sure my body could respond. I had an intense stretching routine, along with a strict diet. Having a regimen on the road would be critical in order to bounce back day after day.

Then, we took a trip by car to scout alternate routes to work my way through Central Florida because it was too dangerous to walk the highway. We went through Pensacola and drove the alternate routes to Orlando. I had timelines to meet with students on the Florida State, University of Florida, Full Sail, University of Central Florida, and Lake Highland Prep campuses. These were all locations where I wanted to do my prayer walk. After Orlando the walking route would be easy to follow because State Road A1A takes you right down to South Beach.

On March 3, 2013, I landed at Pensacola City Hall to start the journey. I had an RV, and each week there would be a different driver from our church who volunteered to travel with me to drive, maintain the RV, cook, and be an overall support that week. He had to either be behind me or in front of me based on where I was going. We spent the nights in Walmart parking lots and RV camps. There had been a small gathering at the church in Orlando to send us. My family was there too, and after a moment of prayer we took off.

On the first day of the walk, when I got out of the RV at Pensacola City Hall, the news media was there to interview me. Someone had tipped them off. The news caught on, and for eleven weeks, from March 3 to May 18, I walked from Pensacola down to South Beach, Miami.

Each week, I had specific cards in a stack of all the principals of the schools, the fire chief, the city council members, the police chief, and others. I had a whole list for each one of the little towns, and that would be my prayer focus for the week. I would also pray for all the churches that I walked by. Even though it was specific to the route, it was an exercise of faith for the entire state. It was great to have had the opportunity to pray with the students on the various campuses. Once in Orlando, I ended up on A1A, heading down through Melbourne, then West Palm, all the way to South Beach. I actually was trying to figure out how to walk through and pray for my hometown

Sarasota, but the routes weren't easy to get across and go down. It would have taken a lot longer. Anyplace that I did not walk through on my route would just be represented by our prayers. I was believing that the Father would bless the whole state. While walking up in the panhandle, I had a vision of a massive storm of destruction heading toward Florida, bringing chaos like we'd never seen before. There were people on the beach completely unaware, enjoying life, doing as they would, having a good time, but they couldn't see the storm brewing. It felt as if that was what was about to hit our state. I remember spending hours crying out as I walked. I said, "Father, would You please have mercy on Florida? Have mercy on us. I pray that You would turn the storm of destruction into a storm of grace." I just kept praying that.

Nine of the weeks I lived on the road, but two of the weeks I was able to go out within an hour's range of home, from Ocala to past New Smyrna, do the walk, and then sleep in my own bed. I would drop a pin marker on the exact spot I stopped at, travel back, and prepare. I would preach Sundays, go back out, and pick up my pin on Monday mornings.

When I started the prayer walk, I encouraged my staff and congregation to do their own prayer walks around the city.

You may remember that in the spring of 2013 there was an attempted mass murder at the University of Central Florida in Orlando. It was national news. What people don't know is that when I started doing my walks, I commissioned my staff to start doing walks around the city of Orlando. We had people stationed on a weekly basis to do walks. Brian Taylor, who's now a pastor in Cincinnati, was our campus pastor at the time. He had a prayer walk on Wednesday nights. On one particular Wednesday the Holy Spirit prompted Brian and said, "Stop. Pray over that dorm." They prayed specifically against murder, depression, and a lot of other things. That weekend was the attempted mass murder.

The story behind it is that the guy had a whiteboard in his room with a list of things to inflict. His plan was to kill as many people as he could. The last point was, "Give 'em hell." He had ammunition, weapons, and a plan. He pulled the fire alarm, and when people started rushing out, his plan was to start picking them off rapid fire. When he came out, other students came out into the quad, and he was trying to kill them, but he couldn't. The gun jammed. After a while, the mayhem of it all unfolded. He panicked, went to his room, and committed suicide. A client of one of our church members, Jose Cruz, who owns a barber shop, was on the front line, investigating mass murders all over the country. Working in special ops, he was part of the investigation at UCF and told Jose that the gun the young man had never jams. That day, that gun jammed because on Wednesday the Holy Spirit said to Brian, "Pray over that dorm." There are kids living today who have no idea it was because of prayer.

During my walk across Florida, we had numerous powerful encounters that could probably be a book in itself. Following are a couple of examples.

STOPPED BY THE POLICE AND HUGGED

On Fridays I would have to get up early, especially when I was further into the panhandle. I wanted to get on the road as soon as I could because I had to go back and preach every weekend. So I'd be working on the message during the week and getting up early. Sometimes it would be dark outside. I would have the RV following behind me with the lights on a couple of early Friday morning occasions. Then, if there was a road that was more of a main highway with 18-wheelers and trucks, the RV was behind me as protection. We didn't do that a lot because it was unsafe for them.

One particular time we had a police officer pass us on the other side of the highway. He saw me walking with an RV behind me, which had to look extremely odd and perhaps alarming, so he made a U-turn to catch up with us. As he got closer to the RV, he turned on his lights, so we were getting pulled over and about to get a ticket. I don't know what for, but this looked odd. I turned around to walk behind the RV to meet the officer, and as I walked toward the RV, I told the driver, "You just stay there." I walked back to the officer and shared what I was doing and asked him how I could pray for him. He went from possibly about to give us a ticket to putting on his lights and escorting us into town. When we got to town, I walked back to the officer behind the RV, and he got out of his car. I don't know if he Googled me or what, but as I was shaking his hand and thanking him for covering us and helping us get to town safely, he looked emotional and thanked me while gripping my hand strongly (he was a muscular guy). I was trying to figure out how to exit this situation because I had a long way to walk. Then he said, "Can I give you a hug?" I said, "Sure." That's easy for me. That guy became my friend.

In fact, on December 4, 2013, I got an email that read, "Pastor Johnson, I don't know if you remember me. When you did your prayer walk, I was the deputy who escorted you into Cross City, Fl. On Nov. 9th I was severely injured in a hunting accident when I fell from a tree. I fractured my right tibia/fibula in several places that required extensive surgery. I know God was watching over me and guided me to the ground. Because by all rights I should be dead. The day I met you was a milestone in my life because it was redirection back towards my Lord and Savior Jesus Christ. I have had several spiritual interactions with pastors and other Godly people prior to my accident. I humbly ask if you would keep me in your prayers. My goal is to return to work and support my family and glorify my God.... Thank You, C.P. Hart."

He kept sending me reports on how he was doing. On July 3, 2016, he said, "Pastor, I led my first Youth to the Lord this week at Camp Anderson in Old Town, Florida. I am also going into the Youth Ministry. By the Grace of God our meeting during your prayer walk through Cross City, Florida was the beginning of an awesome journey. Sincerely, C.P. Hart."

Then, on May 20, 2018, he texted, "Pastor, just a quick word my brother. Just wanted to let you know I'm retiring from the police department June 29th, and I will be accepting a full-time job at Camp Anderson which is a Christian Youth Camp along the Suwannee River. Much Love and Respect. You should come out there and preach sometimes. C.P. Hart."

OLE BOYS WITH A CONFEDERATE FLAG

Another time, I was walking early in the morning. The daylight was coming through, but I still had the RV following me. It was one of those rare occasions. These ole boys were driving down the street on my side of the highway with a huge confederate flag, and the flag blew off into the median. They had to turn around but couldn't at that spot because of the median. The driver dropped off his buddy to pick up the flag, and he kept going to a gas station in front of us and waited. His buddy picked up the flag and had to walk on the side of the road where I was walking. They were ahead of me, and I was watching this whole thing unfold. I was thinking, "Man, this is a good opportunity to show the love of Jesus." He was on the right side of the road and had the flag in his left hand. He didn't see me. I was a bit far away, but I knew I would catch him because I walk at a pretty good pace and he was walking slowly. "Take a picture of this," I told my driver. After catching up to him, I walked up beside him. That had to be the last thing on earth he expected to see, a brother walking on the side of the road in the middle of nowhere. I looked over at him and said, "Hey, man. How are you doing?" I know this was a very odd moment to see me there. I just talked with him about what I was doing. He didn't really respond but was polite and cordial. Then, as we approached the gas station where his friend was waiting in the truck, I said, "May I pray for you?" He allowed me to, and I laid my hand on his shoulder and prayed for him. The picture that was taken shows me walking next to him with the Confederate flag. And I just couldn't help but think, "Man, the Father has a sense of humor." He had also allowed me for a moment to be a picture of grace, reconciliation, love, and kindness in the face of this banner of hate.

AN ENCOURAGING TEXT

At the time of my walk, Pensacola had a high murder rate. Every month, there were several murders, so we prayed against that. On my scouting trip, I was able to visit the church where Lisa Wiggins, whom I got in touch with through a friend in our church, ministered in Pensacola. What was interesting is that on March 29, 2013, during my walk, Lisa texted me.

She said, "Hi, Pastor Johnson. Where are you now, on God's mission?"

"I'm just outside of Perry, Florida," I said, "263 miles covered in prayer so far."

"Several people have asked me that today, and I said I would check. Godspeed continued."

"Thank you, Lisa," I said. "Still believing God for a storm of grace to blow through Pensacola in Jesus' name."

"It already has," she said. "Pensacola has had no murders

this month. Thank God for that. Glory. Thank you, Jesus. Now repentance must come."

"How many murders have y'all been having on a monthly basis?" I asked.

"Last year we averaged two per month," she said, "which does not seem like a lot compared with Chicago or Miami, but it's devastating for us."

That was very encouraging to hear at that time, 263 miles in.

When we finally made it to Miami's South Beach on May 18, 2013, there were about forty people waiting for me who had driven down from Orlando, who had been following. It was our staff, others in the church, and a couple of different pastors from churches in that area who came out. We were huddled up, in a circular form, on the beach. The sky was overcast, and we were celebrating, worshipping, calling out to God, rejoicing, when a holy hush suddenly dropped on us. While we were basking in the silence, hands raised, the clouds shifted, and sunrays shined like a spotlight illuminating us. I remember looking up and seeing one lady who wasn't part of the group, standing there in tears. She didn't even know what was going on, but she was clearly touched. There was a real sense of God's presence on that beach.

This was a snapshot of the entire experience, people on the outside being drawn in by the light and love. Interestingly, the prayer walk never ended. What began with an audible voice on the golf course, an unorthodox divine instruction, had become a reality that touched the state of Florida. We will never know the full impact of our prayers until the other side, though we know some. The experience also transformed the Orlando World Outreach Church into a people of prayer. It united faith in our congregation, that we began a prayer ministry. "Epaphras," wrote Paul, "is always wrestling in prayer for you, that you may stand firm in all the will of God, mature and fully assured" (Col. 4:12). Prayer is dear to the Father's heart, and we became a congregation of Epaphrases. Prayer has become the foundation of what we do. We let the Holy Spirit speak, and we follow. Today, the Orlando World Outreach Church is impacting the globe, starting at home. The Father has continued to call us to so many things. One was to organize and execute He Got Up! events, which helped thousands of homeless people in a variety of ways—providing food and housing, legal services, employment opportunities, and compassionate restorative justice. Over the last couple of years, we've covered over two million dollars in fines, fees, and court costs, and implemented the community service or payment plans for hundreds of individuals in the city. We've been going to Rikers Island Correctional Facility in New York City, bringing hope and healing. After the George Floyd murders, we led thousands of people through the streets of Orlando, reading scripture out loud and the names of Black men and women who have been murdered, calling on the name of the Lord. We marched down Church Street, crossing Division Avenue because it's going to take the church to break the division.

WHAT BEGAN WITH AN AUDIBLE VOICE ON THE GOLF COURSE, AN UNORTHODOX DIVINE INSTRUCTION, HAD BECOME A REALITY THAT TOUCHED THE STATE OF FLORIDA.

This pattern for our church has been the pattern of my life ever since the Father embraced this fatherless boy and started fathering me. He would continue to lead our church and me individually into uncharted waters because the Father longs to reach the orphans and bring them home. Thinking in retrospect, "What does a father do with his child?" one of the most fundamental things he does is teach him how to walk. I was called, and I had to learn how to walk. At first, I literally couldn't walk a mile without getting a blister. That's a stage of becoming a man and a father *in His image*. He taught me how to walk, to bless the state that had schools with powerful alumni who shunned me. That's grace, right? The man with the flag, the schools, all of it. Because here's this state that said, "Forget you. You're out. We're shunning you. You're not going to do what we want? Goodbye." I could have carried so much resentment. The human Tim might have, but I had the Spirit of Jesus giving new life to me. So this whole coming back to Florida feels like it's about grace. Not only am I going to come; I'm going to come back to serve the people here. "The way that You wanted me to serve You back then, with football, wasn't how I was supposed to serve You," I told the Lord. "I needed to go that way so that I could come back and serve You this way."

"I'll Show Up to That"

In 2014 I was at a planning retreat with my guys on staff. One morning I was walking on the treadmill, how I normally do. Again, I felt this impression, vision, weight, presence on me. I couldn't believe what I was feeling and seeing. I had this picture of people broken down, hurting, in wheelchairs, coming out of the ghetto, the woods. They were all rallying together for them to be celebrated and to have a setting where they could hear the gospel but have practical needs met, in a one-step process. He was telling me to merge the massive amount of need with the resources that exist and build a bridge. It was a big event. It was a bit overwhelming as I saw this thing unfold. What made me cry was when Jesus said, "I'll show up to that. I'll show up there." Everything in me believed it could happen, even though it had never happened. When I heard that, *nothing* was going to stop me. "I'll show up to that." I felt

His heart. The Father's heart was, "I'm not looking for another worship service. I'm looking for your worship to become service to those in need." The service to those in need would be marked by the Day of Resurrection. Easter Sunday was the first one.

It took me two years to go across three counties and meet with countless people to build a coalition of the willing CEOs, service providers, educators, employers, technical school directors, moms, dads, lawyers. It ended up being 120 organizations. I started with friends who were visionary leaders. I didn't start by focusing on the church, because I felt as if the church would think I needed something from them when I wanted to do something to bless them. A lot of churches are inundated with so many different needs, so I decided to go to my friends in the corporate world. You can't be a CEO or vice president and not have vision. I spoke with Derek Lewis, who was one of the senior vice presidents of Pepsi. I spoke with Vince LaRuffa, who is an executive with Universal and runs a hotel. I also spoke with Doug Gehret, who is a vice president of Hilton. All three of those guys, in so many words, said, "Let's change the world." They said *yes*. Universal built our original Orlando Serve Foundation He Got Up! website. Still today, anytime we have an event, Derek has Pepsi mobilize resources, and then he has Frito-Lay, anytime we need anything. Doug, with the Hilton, mobilizes the human resources department. Now everybody's involved.

There are hundreds and hundreds of stories. One gentleman, who had a felony on his record, spent years outside of gainful employment. Because of He Got Up! and our connection with mental health providers and others, we had a backdrop to help anybody who needed help. Whoever came to He Got Up! got a golden pass to get interviewed. That meant that anybody who wanted to interview with Hilton on that Tuesday would get a special consideration. The gentleman not only went and got a job but became one of their best employees. It was all because he got another chance.

Another time, a truck driver had lost his license. He wanted to provide for his family. Because of our He Got Up! court, he was able to get his license back. We would take cases, prepare them, go to court, and then resolve them to community service or a payment plan. That whole operation is still going on today. We have story after story after story. We had law enforcement say to one of our team members that he had been on that force for twenty years and had never seen anything like that.

Our church served eight thousand-plus homeless and poor. We hoped for way more, but this was so different that the people it was for didn't really trust it. We did everything we knew. We had fifty-two bus stops and one hundred buses and drove four thousand miles. We would show up personally to a wooded area in Osceola. We went to a lot of different places and personally handed the people the flyers. In fact, there was this one community back then, in Osceola County, where hundreds of people lived in the woods. Outcasts, criminals, ex-offenders, and victims all lived there. We know a lady down in that area who ministers to these people, so we connected with her.

We ended up going to that area and met one guy who was sort of the "mayor" of the woods. His name was Cowboy. My team and I pulled up, and Cowboy was just sitting in the chair. That must've been his routine. It was hot as fire, and he was just sitting there. I think he had a broken hip and shoulder. We interviewed him, and at the end he basically went off about how major shows and networks have come down there and made promises, but none of them came back. He said, "Where's all the money?" I was moved. I took a risk. I said, "Cowboy, what do you want? What can we do for you?" I was thinking, "What did I just say? What am I doing? What if he says, 'I want a house'?" I would just have to figure out how to get it; it is what it is. I was bracing myself for some extreme answer. You know what this man said? He said, "I want a couple pairs of jeans. And I want some shirts and some new shoes. And I want a new tent." I said, "I'll be back." The next week, I rolled up with my crew. He was sitting in the same chair. I went over to him and said, "We're back." We not only got him what he wanted with regard to the clothing, but we got a really nice tent. *Really nice* and *tent* don't seem to go together when you're living in the woods. We tore up his tent. We took his little dresser out and cleaned that whole area up. Then we put the tent up and put his new bed in there. Cowboy came into the tent. He looked around and then got on his knees. I was looking at him, and then I got on my knees with him. He was just thankful. We get a new iPhone, and if it slows down, we're mad. It was a tent. We were about to leave and were going to pray for them. Cowboy started praying, and it was a wrap. We never ended up praying for them; he prayed for us.

Then there was another lady, around the corner, in the woods. Gosh, this tent was horrendous. It had cats running in and out. She was about three hundred pounds. She lived with gangrene legs in a wheelchair. It was bad. We ended up getting her on the bus and bringing her to He Got Up! She got a haircut, got cleaned up, got new clothes, a new wheelchair ordered, and health care. I don't know where she is now, but this was a gateway for everything to change in her life.

One lady who had a seamstress business lost everything in 2008 because a lot of the discretionary income people had kind of went away. That was what her business was built on because it was a luxury to have a seamstress. She struggled, lived hotel to hotel, homeless with her husband and their family. When she came to the He Got Up! court, she got her license back. Her business started to come back a little bit, but she had to take a taxi and get dropped off, and just do the best she could. She shared this at a banquet we had a couple of years ago. At that time, she was living in a home. When you're legitimized in the community, you have options and opportunities. When you're delegitimized, because you don't have any identification, you're in a prison. It's hard to get out. I could go on and on with story after story. It's what the Father does through His people in community and in individual lives.

Jesus said, "I'll show up to that." And He will show up for you too!

CHAPTER 17

PAR FOR THE COURSE

Writing this book was never my intention. I had no desire. The truth is, I've always considered pouring myself out to people and giving my life away was my book. That is exactly what I was doing—going about my business, pastoring an amazing church, fathering my amazing kids, being a husband to an amazing woman, just pouring into people—when the Holy Spirit once again interrupted my life. Like "Prepare to leave," "Clean it up," "You park here," "Plant a church in Orlando," and "Walk across the state," it was another out-of-the-blue, out-of-the-box instruction that was par for the course in how the Lord directs me.

A few years ago, some thirty years after my table encounter where Jesus wrapped His arms around me and then introduced me to the Father, I was back in Pennsylvania speaking at a fundraiser for a fellow Penn Stater and former teammate who was doing youth ministry. My former Penn State roommate D.J. Dozier was there, along with some other old teammates. I've already written about what an exceptionally gifted athlete D.J. was. Drafted in the first round, he had a solid NFL career and was one of the few athletes who played in the NFL and Major League Baseball (MLB). God had used D.J. and his mother back then as I was being directed toward Jesus. As roommates and friends, the two of us grew in the Lord together, and just as the Father had guided me through the

NFL, family life, and ministry, He had done the same with D.J. To this day, he overflows with a contagious love for God and for the lost. The event was a success and afterward turned into a mini reunion of sorts, which was beautiful.

As the room was clearing, a few of us were hanging out, talking. D.J. was standing there, hands in his pocket, looking stoic, expressionless. Randomly, out of nowhere, he said, "Tim, you're gonna write that book." Now, like I said, I had no desire whatsoever to write a book and was actually calculating in my head one more person to ignore. Then D.J. said to me, "I have the title."

I said, "OK, what is it?"

He said, *"Fatherless No More."* When those words came out of D.J.'s mouth, and I'm not exaggerating, I could have fallen down. It hit me like a tidal wave, shaking me to the core, and I have not been able to let it go since. Another thing you need to know is that none of these ideas concerning *Fatherless No More* were ever dominant in any of our conversations. I had never said those words, ever. It was an absolute revelation in the moment to D.J., and I was experiencing a visitation from the Father. The power of God was behind those words when D.J. said them. It was a word from the Father's heart that I don't think I had the capacity to hear from within myself. God had to use someone that I respect and knew didn't play games to speak a piercing word. D.J. describes what happened this way:

> As you were speaking, the Lord spoke to me. That was when I heard the title. It was one of those moments where it wasn't like I was guessing. It was clear as clear can be. That was why I said it to you with such confidence, because I knew it was the Lord. I patiently waited for everybody to get their conversations in with you. Then I said, "Tim, you're going to write that book. I know the title of it." After I told you the title, *Fatherless No More,*

> I remember your reaction. It kind of reminded me of my mom when I told her for the first time what I wanted to do when I was older. She didn't react like I was expecting her to.... But I was excited to find out that you're writing. You're starting to put the pieces together.... You can tell someone something, and it's just a good idea until you realize that it's the Lord. So when I heard the Lord give me the title and I knew precisely this was it, that was a spark. I knew this was not just a good idea. This is a destiny point for God, and for your life.

Now I was standing there around my buddies, totally undone, trying to hold my composure. Inwardly I was thinking, "I don't even know what to do with this." Yet the Father did. All I had to do was be that open conduit for the Holy Spirit to flow through and then follow His lead. As we did all the other times I was given a directive, we began the process of walking it out by faith one step at a time. "Write this book, and get the message of *Fatherless No More* out there." More than a suggestion, it was a mandate. Saying no was not an option, and from the moment I said yes, the enemy has tried to stop it. It's been a struggle, overcoming one obstacle after another, but just as saying no was not an option, neither was giving up.

It's been an incredible journey since that day as the Father through the Holy Spirit has illuminated our every step, right down to the penning of these pages. But more than a book, this is a word from God. Honestly, the world doesn't need another book. What the world needs is a word from God. Ever since receiving the mandate for getting the message of *Fatherless No More* out there, countless souls with bound and broken lives have been set free and are now swimming in the unfathomable depths of the Father's love. He's even opened the door to prisons where the message has been like that warm oil melting so many hardened hearts. We would go in sharing with the detainees, and the corrections officers and corrections officials would get set free as well. That's because quite often those outside the physical bars are locked up in prisons of false freedom. Thinking they are free, they're bound by strongholds, illegitimate identities, and self-defeating patterns, unable to break the cycle. As we've been walking this out, we've seen firsthand the impact the message has had on people. When they heard the words *Fatherless No More*, it evoked all sorts of emotions and reactions in them, further confirming the message.

EVER SINCE RECEIVING THE MANDATE FOR GETTING THE MESSAGE OF *FATHERLESS NO MORE* OUT THERE, COUNTLESS SOULS WITH BOUND AND BROKEN LIVES HAVE BEEN SET FREE AND ARE NOW SWIMMING IN THE UNFATHOMABLE DEPTHS OF THE FATHER'S LOVE.

So just what is the *Fatherless No More* message? You've been reading of my experience of fatherlessness as an infant, growing up with an orphan spirit, and being embraced by Jesus and introduced to the Father in college, and Him fathering me through my life. While I'm far from perfect and fall short in so many ways, one thing I'm certain of is that I am no longer an orphan. I am no longer living out of my pain. I am at peace, knowing that I am loved by the One who created me. Today, when people ask me, "Who is Tim Johnson?" my answer is, "I am loved. I am my Father's son. I am *fatherless no more*." That root identity expresses itself through many other purposes. Yes, I was an NFL player. I am a husband, a father, and a pastor, but I'm living in those things as a loved son, preparing to leave. As a new creation in Christ, I am also loved because the One who made me *is* love. He created me to love Him and to enjoy Him. We know that's the chief end of man.

My hope and goal in *Fatherless No More* is to introduce people to a relationship with heavenly Father through faith in Jesus Christ to know whom they belong to, what to believe, and how to behave for people to be set free from the prisons of false freedom. The false freedom is that "I can make my life what it needs to be," and, "I don't need a father." Every human being needs not just a father but *the Father*. So that absence of knowing whom I belong to, knowing what to believe, and knowing how to behave is a vacuum we try to fill with success, money, relationships, material things, access, and resources. But nothing can replace the voice of the Father. Nothing can replace the freedom that comes through a relationship with Jesus, who brings us back to the Father. We're not free until we're free in Him spiritually. My hope is freedom so people can find their way to knowing the Father's love. The sacrifice He gave through His Son, Jesus, was to redeem us, not to judge us, punish us, or take away our toys.

Regardless of our good, bad, or absent relationship with earthly fathers there is a freedom we get from knowing the heavenly Father through Jesus Christ that we cannot get from anyone or anything else. Whether your father was absent or present, we are all impacted by this one relationship. God uses many words to describe Himself, but one is stunningly personal—Father. This is thrilling—and problematic. We don't have another Jesus or another Holy Spirit, but we do have another father, our earthly one, and our experience with him changes the way we see God.

THREE BASIC NEEDS EVERY PERSON HAS

A key foundational truth in this *Fatherless No More* message is that every person, whether male or female, has three basic needs. If these needs are not met, or are somehow distorted, we tend to reach for false attachments that develop into false or illegitimate identities and counterfeit lifestyles. These false attachments always promise what they can never ultimately deliver. They may start out giving us what we think we want or need, but eventually they leave us void, addicted, anxious, fearful, depressed, trapped, unfulfilled, and locked up in emotional prisons. To avoid that, God has built three basic needs into our human makeup:

1. the need to know to whom we belong

2. the need to know what to believe

3. the need to know how to behave

Who or what we see ourselves belonging to tells us what to believe and how to behave. For example, if a young man on the streets has a gun and belongs to a gang, that gang mentality will become his identity and he will behave accordingly, regardless of the consequences. His affirmation, self-worth, and rewards will come from belonging to the group. Breaking free is difficult and requires the power of the Spirit of the Father rising up in people to stand against the forces and people imprisoning them.

In the same way, if I'm in the C-suite club on Wall Street, and I actually belong to my job, all the rewards, affirmations, and dynamics of achieving in that arena, I will believe it's my life and will behave accordingly. Whatever it is—a gang, corporate America, the NFL, even the ministry—whatever we feel we belong to becomes our identity and the source of our existence. Many of those things are not bad in themselves. We touched on this earlier, that careers are wonderful and needed. Being an accomplished athlete is a great achievement. Belonging to groups is good, and ministry is admirable. Still, for true peace and fulfillment, your identity has to be defined from the original source of your existence and living in that connection. Jesus told the woman at the well, "Everyone who drinks this water will be thirsty again, but whoever drinks the water I give them will never thirst. Indeed, the water I give them will become in them a spring of water welling up to eternal life" (John 4:13–14). After five ended marriages, this woman had been living in so much dysfunction, brokenness, and pain, feeling used, abused, and dirty. Mostly, though, life had left her dry and parched. Yet instead of condemning her and giving her "ten steps to a better you," Jesus offered her living water that would satisfy the deepest thirst within her soul. He offered her Himself. Jesus was *the well* sitting on a well. When you know who you are and whose you are, your thirst is quenched. You can rest knowing you are loved and do life at the pace of grace. You may still have goals and a strong work ethic, except now there will be a calm, quiet confidence and satisfaction in your soul that will actually enhance your performance. You will *have* these things, but these things will not "have" you. You will be living your life "preparing to leave."

I remember my last year playing with the Bengals. I had been in the league for almost a decade, and there was a rookie defensive lineman who was drafted pretty high coming into camp. He was an incredibly gifted athlete who left college early because several NFL teams had expressed interest. The Bengals snagged him, and his room at training camp was right across from mine. Wanting to welcome him, I went over to his room to chat.

"I remember you," he said almost immediately. "I grew up in DC while you were playing for the Redskins."

That made me feel really old. I was thirty at the time, and he couldn't have been more than twenty or twenty-one. We were talking, chopping it up, getting to know one another, when all of a sudden, the Holy Spirit rose up inside me to ask him one simple question. I looked him square in the eyes and asked, "Why are you here?"

"What?" he responded, a bit taken aback. Then he continued, "Man, I'm here to play ball and make money. That's what it's all about. They both go together."

"That's not what I mean," I said. "Why are you here on this earth?"

I could see the question hit him way harder than expected. He was really giving it some serious thought. "I don't know," he finally admitted, transparently. And for the next forty-five minutes he was like a sponge soaking up the gospel of Jesus Christ as I shared it with him. Before I had even finished, he leaped out of his chair, totally unsolicited, fell on his knees, and started repenting. At that point, all I did was lead this young man in a prayer to put his trust in Jesus. And let me tell you something, when he rose from his knees, he was a different man. The transformation was instant and real. It's amazing how God does that. It's supernatural. The next day, again with zero prompting from me, he took all his drug paraphernalia, ungodly music, and other things like that—every bit of it—and threw them in a dumpster. My goodness. All that began from asking one question: "Why are you here?"

Until the Father's love filled his core, my young teammate had no idea what his purpose for being on this planet was, except in his *doing things* and his pursuit of pleasure. Now, as a loved son of the Father's, he could play ball with a brand-new identity. He could have a great career while preparing to leave. He wasn't locked in a prison of false freedom.

When our core identity is anything other than the One who created us and gave us life, we miss the mark. Never ultimately fulfilled, we place our faith in substitutes like self-medication, an unhealthy drivenness to succeed, sexual addiction, and other enslaving practices. We give ourselves to these counterfeit reasons for existence, believing they are our answer to the longings inside us, and it's locking us up like prisoners, impacting our behavior, even if that behavior is self-defeating. The damage it's reeking in our lives is obvious, yet we are powerless to change. What's insane is all the while, we've convinced ourselves that we are free. This is the prison of false freedom. We ignore the warning lights in our souls, and as time passes, the bars around us become thicker. To unlock the door that leads out of bondage to authentic freedom, those three questions must be answered, ideally as a child, or eventually as an adult. If they are not answered in our early years, we are going to live a counterfeit lifestyle, carry wounds and insecurities into adulthood, affecting other relationships.

"A father to the fatherless" (Ps. 68:5), the Father is the One who defines whom we belong to and what we believe. He is the One who defines how we behave, even cleaning up locker rooms and negotiating contracts. If you don't have that, you will be lost, feeling like an orphan and living out of your pain more often than not.

LIVING OUT OF OUR PAIN

Ideally, a person's life should not be derailed based on the actions or nonactions of their natural father. Unfortunately, that's not the case. The cuts from father wounds run deep and with a two-edged blade. They slice the hearts of individuals, which impacts the culture as a whole because people tend to live out of their pain. Satan has done a masterful job of using the issues of fatherlessness to derail our society. The whole world has been stung by the curse of fatherlessness. That's because fatherlessness is at the root of hell itself. But there is something else critically important that we must understand. The devastation, depravity, and deviant behavior in this world didn't come from our biological fathers. What do I mean by that, and why is it important? It's because Satan has also done a powerful work of capturing people based on what their father did or didn't do. Many times the way we view our earthly fathers directly impacts how we live and how we view God the Father.

If you look at prison stats, they are overwhelming. The sobering statistics don't lie. Seventy percent of juveniles in state-operated institutions and 85 percent of youths in prisons come from fatherless homes; 80 percent of rapists come from fatherless homes; 63 percent of youth suicides come from fatherless homes; 95 percent of those on death row hated their fathers.[1] What this illustrates is that when we are out of alignment with our earthly fathers, the anger and pain inside us manifests in our behavior. Again, for some it is criminal behavior; for others, most of us, it is an internal struggle that manifests itself in a myriad of unhealthy ways. Mainly, we live out of our pain. In my case it was building walls of self-protection and self-sufficiency, determining not to need anyone, and treating women like objects.

When we don't know to whom we belong and we don't know our purpose, we don't know how to live. That's not a good place to be.

A PROPHETIC CONFIRMATION

I'd like to share a supernatural prophetic story here that confirms the message of *Fatherless No More* in a profound way. It involves a woman named Tina Campbell of the multi-Grammy Award-winning gospel duo Mary Mary, her sister, Erica Campbell, being the other half. It's important to note that Tina lives in California, and I live in Florida. At the time of our first interaction, we had never met or had any previous contact. Like most people, I had only heard of the sister duo through their music. On Thursday, April 22, 2021, early in the morning, I was upstairs in my house praying, "Father, show me the secrets of Your heart. Is there anyone that needs to be healed? Anyone that You have a message for?" At 7:40 a.m., out of nowhere this strong impression came about Tina of Mary Mary, which is reaching the world. I quickly recorded the message as the Holy Spirit downloaded it to me. The word was so jarring and specific that I thought, "Lord, let this be You."

Then, at 10:39 a.m., I had another download for Tina, which I recorded. Later that afternoon, I dropped Le'Chelle off at the airport, and when I got back to the house, intercession for Tina to be healed hit me with groaning, tears, and praying in tongues. I knew I had to be obedient and find a way to somehow get the message to her. My connection was singing legend and multiple-Grammy Award-winner CeCe Winans, who is a friend of our family from our time in Nashville and also acquainted with Tina in the music industry. I called CeCe and told her I had a word for Tina Campbell and asked if she would simply relay the message. Not long afterward Tina and I were on the phone together, and the Father showed up in a mind-blowing way. That conversation led to a long-term relationship where the Father continued to show up and bring lasting change. Following is the actual word I gave her and then Tina's response. Consistent with the others, they are raw and real.

THE WORD

7:40 a.m. download: "Tina is having a breakdown. But it's not her mind or body. It's her will. I want her to surrender her will completely to Me. And I will release healing into her mind, and the abuse she has suffered in the past will no longer define her future. And I will repay those who hurt her. I want to free her from regret, from unforgiveness and bitterness, which will defile all that I have planned for her. She will no longer fear good news turning to bad news, because My good news for her will last forever. My mighty hand of deliverance is upon her to deliver her and to move through her to bring deliverance to many multitudes with great power and anointing. It will not be her. It will be Me who does this, and no man can do what I do. She will worship Me from the depths of her being because of the outpouring and refreshing of My presence. She will see the beauty of My Son, Jesus, in and through her life. I'm closing doors that need to be closed and opening new doors to My ways into the work I've called her to do. First John 4:18 talks about there [being] no fear in love. I am enough for you. As your Father, I have rescued you from being an orphan who seeks to perform for approval, because My approval of you comes from how My Son performed on the cross. I approve of you without your performance. I am drawing you closer to Me for you to experience the resting place of My love. You belong to Me, and I belong to you. I want you to enjoy being with Me, as I enjoy being with you. I will seal my Word in your heart so it will never be lost, and you will be made whole. I love you forever."

10:39 a.m. download: "Tina has deep father wounds that have never healed. She feels abandoned, not because people don't love her but because she doesn't trust their love. It's hard to tell the difference between those who really love her and those who said they loved her but abused her mentally and emotionally, physically. It's like a pet that has been treated harshly. It makes the pet scared around people, even when they just want to love the pet. That's the picture I got. The father wants to heal those wounds by healing your heart from the wound of unforgiveness."

Tina's Response

Pastor Tim, whom I now call my "pastor dad," called me and told me everything about my life, that you had to be either God, my mother, my husband, or one of my blood sisters that I talked to, to know. So I knew this was from God. I mean, it was spot on. Like when he said, "Tina is having a breakdown." I was over here breaking down. And then the part about my father, and me feeling fatherless, and I don't trust anyone's love, and many more things. A random person would not know that. On the outside I have a very successful career. And I'm a very encouraging person to many people in the world because of the music and platform that God has given me. You wouldn't know everything my songs are saying; I'm struggling with it at this point in time in my life. You wouldn't know that there's so much hell going on in my house with the turmoil in the relationships because the devil is trying to destroy something that God's trying to build. You wouldn't know. You just wouldn't know all the specifics of my life that pastor was saying unless God was putting those things there.

It got me at my core because I was just broken down. Just prior to CeCe calling me saying Pastor Tim had a word, I had been crying out and praying to God. I was like, "I need some help. I need like a coach, I need somebody to walk with me, like, you know, I'm in this space. I'm in this funk. And I've been in it for quite a while, and I can't seem to get out of it. I need somebody who's spiritually stronger and more experienced, and I don't know, closer with God to help me because I want to be close." I kid you not, that's what I was praying. And Pastor Tim, who became "pastor dad," was exactly whom I needed. After our call, he prayed with me on a weekly, sometimes daily, basis. After giving me the word from the

Lord, he prayed with me and rebuked me. He silenced the enemy that was talking. But it was all through a spirit of humility and love. I mean, he helped me and my husband, individually. He even flew out here with his wife and committed time and days to just walking us through deliverance and maturation in God. I needed clarity and more revelation and more understanding. I needed somebody to care enough to impart some things into me that I had not received, or maybe had not been ready to receive. He helped me understand about my orphan spirit—that is when you don't feel you belong, when you don't exactly know who you are in terms of a sense of belonging, when you don't fully understand who you are in terms of being the embodiment of the love of God and being His daughter. A lot of us say, "Oh, I'm a child of God, and I'm a daughter of God." But when you really understand what that means, everything about your existence exudes that on your greatest days and your worst of days, when you know that you belong, when you know that you are loved, when you know that you don't have to act, you don't have to *do*; you just have to *be*. When you know that, there's a different confidence in your life, there's a difference in how you recover from things. There's a difference in how you respond rather than react to the challenges that life sends your way. And Pastor helped me to understand those things and understand that I am the loved of God. I am His daughter, no matter my flaws or my shortcomings. God loves me. He's pleased with me. Pastor helped me to understand that until you are more interested in God's will and God's way, you're gonna be stuck with your way and in this condition that you're in. You have to trust and love God your Father enough to accept His way and His timing for what He wants and what He has for you. Every single time I talked to pastor, he addressed me "Woman of the Most High God." When I reacted by saying ungodly and dishonorable things because my circumstances had overcome me, he would still call me "Woman of the Most High God." He continued to remind me who I am in the Lord, so much so that I started believing it, and nobody had ever beat me over the head so consistently with, "You are still the woman of God. You are still loved by God. You're still important to Him. I don't care what your flaws are, what stage of immaturity you're going through, and whatever it is that you're trying to evolve to, who you are and what you are is loved by Him."

FATHER WOUNDS

My daddy is dead. And my daddy was a great man of God, but a flawed man. One flaw was that my dad had favorites. After my brother died, he tried seven more times to get a son, I think because my dad always wanted sons— someone to hold the family name in his image. And because he didn't get that, he was a bit preferential to the sisters that looked like him. I didn't and was always fighting for attention and looking for value. I definitely was loved by my father. But he had favorites, so I found myself always thinking that I needed to perform to earn value. I knew my father loved me but didn't feel he liked me. I realized as I got older that it had affected me for many years. I had this orphan-like approach to life— like I wasn't truly valued and always had to perform to be someone worth accepting. I couldn't just be myself. But when you have a sense of belonging and know who you are and know that you are loved and accepted and received, you don't do that; those were orphan-like practices. I had a lot of that orphan-like spirit that you see in fatherless people. People that have loving fathers who have that validation and affirmation, they act differently.

They don't have to prove who they are. They're just confident in being themselves and being loved. I even see a difference in the three sisters that were my father's favorites. There's a confidence they exude where they don't have to prove themselves. I really had to fight to prove myself all the time. With *fatherless no more*, Pastor walked me through all the things that I just explained. It helped me to understand you're not fatherless, and you don't have to perform to be loved and accepted and received. Because you are; you just don't know it. You need to be reminded of that. He helped me to understand I was not fatherless, that I was not only loved by my heavenly Father, but I was loved by my natural father. I don't have to keep performing to be loved. Pastor helped me to understand that when you don't know you are loved by the Father, you just feel pressure to perform. You can't just rest in who you are. Now I know that I am no longer fatherless, and I can just be me and can be content with that. And whenever I can't seem to do, the Father has me covered. I know I'm covered and I'm not alone. When you're fatherless, you feel like you're alone. Like I gotta have my own back. I gotta have the answers. When it all comes down to it, it's just me. But when you are connected to the Father, it ain't ever just me. I'm loved. I'm valuable to somebody—not just somebody; I'm valuable to the Father of all creation, the One who made everything. I'm important to Him. I'm His daughter no matter what I've done, no matter what I don't do, no matter what I've accomplished, no matter what I have not been able to evolve to. I'm still fathered and loved because He just chose to love me like that. He created me, and He just loves me, period. Because He wants to. I may have struggles in the Christian world, but one thing I know—that I'm loved. Now I don't battle or struggle with that. I don't have to fit into this or that space or accomplish this or that to be accepted by those around me. Before I was like, if I mess up, I can be out of God's good graces. If I mess up too much, I might be thrown away. One thing I know for sure now is I will never be thrown away by my Daddy who loves me. I'm gonna always be important to Him, no matter what. No matter if I honor him or not, no matter if I please Him or not. I may not be used by Him. I may miss out on some of the opportunities that He had for me if I don't choose to comply and live my life surrendered. But I will always be loved by Him and valuable to Him. Pastor taught me until I got it. Because I would have it, and then I would lose it. And then I would have it, and then I would lose it. And then I will believe it. And then life circumstances will come. And then I would think that maybe not so much. Now I think I finally messed up. Now I think I lost it. No, no, no, no, no, I'm not going to ever lose the love of my Father. And I'm not going to ever lose the value that my Father has placed on me because it has less to do with me and more to do with Him. I'm His because He chose me. I'm loved by Him because that's what He chose. That was His original design and idea of me before I ever became. So there's nothing that I can do to mess it up. Pastor helped me to understand that.

Let this prophetic word become your own. It was a message to Tina, but it's really to all of us. Grab hold of it and run with it. You're loved by Him because that's what He chose. It was His plan!

On the flip side of Tina's story, you could have had a wonderful earthly father and still be an orphan in spirit if you do not know the Father. There was a lady in our church put together to the nines. I mean, she looked as though she just walked straight out of a magazine. She and her husband had a wonderful family. What none of us knew, or would have ever guessed, was that every night she would get sloppy drunk in her house. It got to the point where one day her husband found her on the floor in a very debilitating condition. I got the call to go meet with her. It's important to note here that Le'Chelle and I had a great relationship with them. So we were a little shocked when we found this out. Eventually, it came out through counseling that her main issue was that she was still mourning her father's death, though it had been some time. There were other issues, but this was the major one and catalyst. She did not know how to handle his leaving, because he had been such a great dad, an idol to her.

He was everything to this woman, who was his little daughter. It was a beautiful story of a father and a daughter loving each other. But when he was gone, she didn't know how to function, and I had to help her understand that a good father is a gift from the Father. No father, however—a good one or a bad one—should be a period in your life. They shouldn't end the story of your identity, because every earthly father is supposed to point their children to the ultimate Father in heaven. And if I don't know Him, and my earthly father is out of the picture, I no longer know to whom I belong. This woman didn't know whom to believe in, and her behavior demonstrated that she was lost. Good fathers and great fathers are a blessing. We need more of them, but as a father you don't understand true fatherhood until you understand that the child you have cannot see you as the ultimate source. You are *a* source, but there's a difference between being *a* source and being *the* source.

A source can change vessels, but *the* source of your existence, and that you belong to Him, never changes. On the other hand, if you had the worst father in the world but know the heavenly Father, He will become a Father for you. Some say, "My father was so horrific that I wish I never had a father!" Those accounts are no different. The effects are the same. In both cases those fathers are not the period. They are commas, which means there is a continuation. Whatever your earthly father was or was not, great or horrible, he' s a comma, not a period. By comma I don't mean moving on from the relationship unless there's abuse. We need closeness with our fathers, if possible. Ideally, we have a strong and balanced relationship with them, but at some point we have to understand our ultimate security and identity is in our heavenly Father, who created us and calls us into completeness in Him. Without that completeness we will always be incomplete. There's a phrase that we've used about how there's a hole in the soul of every child in the shape of their dad. When we're born and that man is not there, or he is around but absent, we try to fill that hole in our soul with other things that don't satisfy. As you will see, Adam made us orphans, creating a hole in our soul for our eternal Father—and until that hole is filled with Him, we will live out of our pain even if we are denying it. Yet Jesus came to make us *fatherless no more.*

PART II

YOUR PATHWAY
TO FREEDOM

Without a relationship with the Father, and being defined by the Father, there is a false mindset that has held you hostage, in emotional prison, much like the stark realities of a physical prison. Yet the Word of God tells us that freedom comes where there is truth (John 8:32) and truth is the key that unlocks the prison doors. We need not fear this new liberty, because the Father—who loves us more than we love ourselves—promises to walk the path with us, holding our hands as we go.

Interestingly, in my process of developing the Fatherless No More message and witnessing its impact on people, a Holy Spirit blueprint, so to speak, has emerged to help us better understand truth and apply it directly to our lives. It's a pathway leading to freedom called "The Five A's": acceptance, affirmation, agreement, accountability, and access. The truths brought forth in each of these principles will help you define who you are and then how to move forward, with the Holy Spirit's wisdom, on a path that creates freedom in you. The Father's desire is to free you and then remake you from the inside out. These Five A's cut through the facades of suppression and dismissal that are keeping you from fully engaging the Father. He's giving you the keys of truth to unlock your prison door, but you have to turn them and choose to walk out the door and follow the pathway to further freedom and life.

CHAPTER 18

THE FIRST A: ACCEPTANCE

It seems golf courses are a place where the Father meets me on a regular basis. This time I was knocking some balls around the course with a successful businessman. Great guy, but it was evident that his identity was completely wrapped up in his business. That's pretty much all he talked about. At some point between tee shots, I asked him, "Hey, man, can you tell me who you are? I mean, strip away from you every piece of what you just announced as your identity while existing on this piece of dirt spinning in space." You know what this brilliant businessman told me? His guard dropped and he said, "I don't know. I really don't know."

Usually when I ask people, "Who are you?" I get a wide range of answers. "I play ball." "I'm a doctor." "A teacher." "Mother." "I don't know who I am." Many different answers. Christians will often respond, "Well, I'm a child of God." And that's a solid answer. As believers we are His children. But guess what? There's an identity that's even more powerful than being a child of God.

While so many people identify with being a son or daughter of God, they still struggle with not *feeling* loved. They perpetually beat themselves up, deeming themselves undeserving of His love while living in false guilt, condemnation, or the pain of the past. To experience and live in the freedom of His complete *acceptance*, your foundation must be rooted in the fact that the

189

Father created you for the express purpose of unconditionally loving you.

Going back to Adam, try to imagine the Father's pair of celestial hands methodically beginning to scoop up the loose ground on His freshly created earth, moving it into a pile. When a sufficient amount had been placed in the pile, His hands began to arrange and sculpt the dirt around carefully. When the mound of earth had been fashioned into the desired form, the Father bent down, looked with approval at the shape, and placed His mouth over the earthen lips of the form. He breathed, forcing air into the vessel He had fashioned. Suddenly, miraculously, the form responded to the breath and sprang to life. "The LORD God formed the man of dust from the ground and breathed into his nostrils the breath of life, and the man became a living creature" (Gen. 2:7, ESV). Adam was aware that he was the culmination and climax of creation, an experience of unconditional love, and that the Creator had just formed a special bond with him—a relationship of love. How do we know it was a relationship of love? Consider this: "God *is* love" (1 John 4:8, emphasis added). Love is a Person, and this love created us in His image (Gen. 1:27).

Another important note is Adam was basically useless, just there when God breathed into him. All he did was receive. Everything about Adam came from and out of the Father. Now, fast-forward through time. Jesus was breathing life into a lifeless, useless world. God the Father did it again, in a very familiar way. He breathed Jesus into existence as God made flesh, that whoever believes in Him won't perish in the dust but have everlasting life (John 3:16). This is the greatest, the purest, the most fulfilling love in existence. And this love wants you to experience acceptance.

That's how Adam came alive, and it's the only way we're going to come alive.

But don't miss this critical part: Adam was on the ground, and he was accepted. While he was useless, the Father breathed His life into him and gave Adam the identity of being unconditionally loved out of the expression of the One who was perfect love. You don't know what acceptance is until you've had an encounter with perfect love, the Creator of your soul, breathing His breath into you. God's love was sent into this world to give you and me an opportunity to feel the acceptance of divine love. Because God *is* love, you can't separate the two. And when we have been loved by Him, there is no more separation between us and God because of our sin; the gap is filled. Nothing can get into it. Now, if I am separated from the Father, fear can be put in that gap. Unbelief can be put in, as well as anger, money, or sex. In fact, you can put all kinds of things to try to fill that gap of our separation. But when love binds us together, the gap closes. It is unconditional love. And there is no fear in perfect love. "There is no fear in love; but perfect love casts out fear, because fear involves torment. But he who fears has not been made perfect in love" (1 John 4:18, NKJV). Surprisingly, the opposite of fear is not faith. It's perfect love—not just love, but perfect love. I'm fearful. I'm trapped. I'm bound by all kinds of things. And in comes the rescuer, the deliverer of me from me. And it's perfect. *Acceptance* is about perfect love and the experience that's available through Jesus with that perfect love.

MOST PEOPLE DON'T REALIZE HOW MUCH THEY ARE *LOVED* UNTIL THEY HAVE AN ENCOUNTER WITH GOD'S ALL-CONSUMING AND UNCONDITIONAL LOVE.

For many people, love is conditional. Conditions must be met to "earn" our love. This attitude stands in stark contrast to God's unconditional love, which never ceases, never fails.

"The steadfast love of the LORD never ceases; his mercies never come to an end" (Lam. 3:22, ESV). "I trust in God's unfailing love for ever and ever" (Ps. 52:8). Unfailing. The Father doesn't know how to fail. He can be relied on in times of need.

Unconditional love does not mean God loves everything we do, but rather His love is so intense that He loves every sinner, no matter how vile and despicable he or she may be in the eyes of humanity, so much that through what Jesus did at the cross He provides a way for them to find love, life, and holiness (John 3:16).

Most people don't realize how much they are loved until they have an encounter with God's all-consuming and unconditional love. I didn't. His love is not human love. Seventy times seven is not human. We can't forgive like that unless supernaturally empowered by the Holy Spirit. Each time He washes us, the Holy Spirit does a work in us. In this process of washing and renewal, of seventy times seven, little by little He is conforming us to the image of Jesus. It's a lifetime process. This is one of the reasons the enemy comes against us with lies. "Come on, now. You can't go back to God again. Do you really think He's going to forgive you again? How could He? You sinned with your eyes wide open. He's angry and disappointed in you. Just give up." It's another lie. Titus wrote, "For the grace of God has appeared that offers salvation to all people. It teaches us to say 'No' to ungodliness and worldly passions, and to live self-controlled, upright and godly lives in this present age" (Titus 2:11–12). God the Father's grace teaches us how to live and *behave*. That includes learning to accept His ongoing gift of forgiveness for us, then trusting the Holy Spirit to lift us up to help us in our pursuit of obedience and learning how to forgive others.

Human beings like to try to match the Father's unconditional love by loving people through difficult times. This is good. However, even those who strive to love unconditionally fall short of the 1 Corinthians 13 standard of love. "Love is patient, love is kind. It does not envy, it does not boast, it is not proud. It does not dishonor others, it is not self-seeking, it is not easily angered, it keeps no record of wrongs. Love does not delight in evil but rejoices with the truth. It always protects, always trusts, always hopes, always perseveres" (1 Cor. 13:4–7). We strive for this, but none of us hit the mark perfectly. However, the Father always does. This is God's perfect love for us. When Jesus told Peter to forgive those who sinned against him seventy times seven, He wasn't saying forgive 490 times and cut it off (Matt. 18:22). No. He was saying to always forgive. Jesus would never tell us to do something that He doesn't do. And Jesus only did what He first saw the Father do. This is huge. The implication is we forgive in unlimited measure, because we've been forgiven in unlimited measure. Holocaust survivor Corrie ten Boom said it well: "To forgive is to set a prisoner free and to discover the prisoner was you." She understood well. Forgiveness doesn't mean accepting certain behavior or continuing to allow abuse or being used. It means we are releasing that person to love others and move on with life while out of our heads. That may be with or without us.

So how do we take the step into understanding *acceptance* when we feel rejected and the picture the Father is showing us contrasts our feelings? What would it do for us if we could actually embrace that we are accepted regardless of our circumstances and failures?

I Belong

We all have a need to belong and to be seen. *Acceptance* says, "I belong." Most every place that I have to belong to is going to cost me. But with the Father, it gets flipped.

Jesus Himself is one of the most potent examples of acceptance.

Before His public ministry started, when John the Baptist was baptizing people in the Jordan River, Jesus was also baptized. When He came up out of the water, heaven was opened, and the Holy Spirit descended upon Him in bodily form like a dove. That's when the voice of the Father came out of heaven and said, "This is my Son, whom I love; with him I am well pleased" (Matt. 3:17). Then, when Jesus was led into the wilderness to be tempted, it was knowing whom He belonged to that enabled Him to say no to Satan's offers. And the Father's words of acceptance here also came before any performance from Jesus. No work. No message. No miracle, or wonder, or healing. Nothing. He had done nothing but be a Son who knew He was loved by His Father. All of us long to hear the words "That's my boy!" or, "That's my girl!" for just being who we are.

TURN ON THE FAUCET

When you turn on a faucet, you expect water to come out, not mud or oil. When it does, how much water did the faucet create? None. The faucet was simply available for the water to flow through. Similarly, Jesus is telling us to be a faucet, a branch, when He says, "Abide in Me, and I in you. As the branch cannot bear fruit of itself, unless it abides in the vine, neither can you, unless you abide in Me" (John 15:4, NKJV). Jesus was saying the virtue of fruit in your life is only going to come from Him—not your past, pain, or personal pleasure. I've never seen a branch force itself to be fruitful. It simply stays connected. It's the life in the vine. When connected to the Father, the source of what's coming out of our faucets is the love of the Father through Jesus in the power of the Holy Spirit. What we're doing is learning how to unclog our faucets because the culture, people, and we will jam things in them, creating blockages that keep the Holy Spirit of Jesus from flowing. Lust, anger, pride, shame, guilt, loneliness, unforgiveness, and bitterness are just some of the things we allow to clog our faucets. But the Father made you to be like a faucet, freely allowing the fullness of who He is to flow through you, the love that surpasses knowledge. This is the reason you start with "Who am I?" I'm loved. I don't even understand it, but I'm loved by the One who made me. I'm going to start there and allow myself to get unclogged so that now what flows out of me as a son, daughter, father, athlete, and friend is His love.

As long as Adam stayed in union with the Father, he couldn't mess it up because the faucet was flowing into divine authority, divine freedom, divine power. There were no hindrances, no barriers to divinity. Man and Maker dwelled together in the garden life. As we've pointed out, in Adam's free will, he eventually chose to separate himself, and the flow got cut off. Suddenly, they saw themselves naked and covered themselves. There was now shame where there had been none. Jesus came in the "fullness of the time" (Gal. 4:4), which means God's perfect time in world history, to reconnect us so divine love could once again flow through us.

However, sometimes we need dams to break, and there's only one force strong enough. It's the Father's love through His Son, Jesus Christ. It will unjam all the reasons that were blocking your flow of living water. "He who believes in Me," declared Jesus, "as the Scripture has said, out of his heart will flow rivers of living water" (John 7:38, NKJV).

Our central purpose is to live in that flow of living water—and you can because you're accepted. He paid the price for you to be, and it was high. He did it because the Father "so loved the world." "The world" means you and me. Jesus was rejected so we could be accepted (John 1:10–12). "Accept one another, then, just as Christ accepted you, in order to bring praise to God" (Rom. 15:7). It's not an *acceptance* based on whether someone accepted our behavior. If you choose Him by faith, you're accepted.

CHAPTER 19

THE SECOND A: AFFIRMATION

During my second year with the Pittsburgh Steelers, I was young and still amazed that I was in the NFL, but I was even more amazed that I was living this new life with the Father in His presence. One day before hitting the road for training camp, Le'Chelle, Christa, and I were having breakfast at a restaurant. I'd trained hard and felt physically that I was at the elite level. With a year behind me, I understood what it was going to take to succeed and had upped my training to that intensity. Yet the whole time we were eating that morning a strange uneasiness was stirring inside me. I was sitting there wondering what was wrong because physically I was prepared. Le'Chelle figured it was just those normal pre-camp butterflies; however, a deeper issue was going on that was hard to articulate, even to my wife. Something was missing, but I couldn't pinpoint what. I was looking around. Le'Chelle was fine. Christa was fine. The bills were paid. Everybody was healthy. Physically, I was ready to go do my job at a high level. I was living my dream. Grateful. Honored. Committed. I was now living as a son. So why was I feeling this void? I tried to explain it to Le'Chelle the best I could and then drove on to camp.

I couldn't have been on the road for thirty minutes when the Spirit of God showed up in my vehicle. I got so overwhelmed by His visitation that I was shaking and crying and had to pull off the road. When I did, it felt as if Jesus were sitting

197

in the seat next to me. It was then I heard the Holy Spirit say, "I'm with you. You're *mine*. I see you. I'm proud of you." With that came a sense that the Father was accepting and affirming me. There was peace and freedom and release. I had not even been praying for it and didn't know I needed it. With the *affirmation*, the emotional and verbal support, the emptiness disappeared. What I needed to hear that day is something every one of us needs to hear—a father, *the* Father, saying, "I love you for you. I'm proud of you. You're *mine*."

IT WAS THEN I HEARD THE HOLY SPIRIT SAY, "I'M WITH YOU. YOU'RE MINE. I SEE YOU. I'M PROUD OF YOU."

When God walked with Adam and Eve in the garden during the cool of the day, it became their greatest source of pleasure. In His presence is fullness of joy, wrote the psalmist (Ps. 16:11). Every need they could have possibly wanted was met. It was a place of intense heights of contentment and peace. Every emotion was affected, every desire satisfied. There was perfect health, along with rest of spirit and soul in bodies and minds that never fatigued. I'm reminded of my encounter at the table back at Penn State. In that moment of intense love and peace with the warm oil of His presence pouring over me, time ceased, and I never wanted to leave that place, ever. I can only imagine Adam and Eve living in that perpetual state as they went through their daily routines.

The garden was a place of perfect pleasure and fellowship with the Father—then something happened. There were two trees in the garden, the tree of life and the tree of the knowledge of good and evil. Adam and Eve were given explicit instructions not to eat from the latter, so I'm sure every time they passed, the fruit and what it represented enticed their senses and they had to make the choice to obey God. They were given free will because love is impossible without freedom to choose. All was good until Satan came in and offered Adam and Eve, by proxy, a chance to be like God. The serpent told Eve, "God knows that your eyes will be opened as soon as you eat it, and you will be like God, knowing both good and evil" (Gen. 3:5, NLT). The problem with that is they were already like God in so knowing only good. There was nothing new for Satan to offer them except the knowledge of evil.

The curiosity to understand what God clearly didn't want them to understand, and then to agree with Satan's deception on God's command, caused Adam, with his free will, to rebel. Sin entered the world. Adam and Eve exited paradise, and they became spiritually homeless. The divine economy of the whole universe was disrupted. Earth was groaning now because of sin. Interestingly, when the Father saw this, He groaned as well. Adam's sin broke His heart. I don't think most people have an adequate grasp of the seriousness of sin and the absolute holiness of God.

It's not that Adam and Eve committed this little act of disobedience and God was super harsh with a big stick waiting to pop them. No. It was like putting a couple of drops of toxic cyanide in a glass of the absolute purest water. It contaminates and makes the pure polluted, even deadly.

It's important to note here that the consequences of the fall were unleashed in the spirit realm before they were ever seen in the natural world. Though Adam and Eve instantly died spiritually, it took time for them to die physically. Spiritual death always leads to physical death. All of us are born spiritually dead until we are born again and infused with life from the Father. Jesus said, "I have come that they may have life, and that they may have it more abundantly" (John 10:10). There is no life until Jesus gives it to us from the Father. This infused spiritual life also defeats our physical death. "O death, where is thy sting? O grave, where is thy victory?" (1 Cor. 15:55).

It must have been heart-wrenching for the Father when Adam chose to believe Satan over Him. But what did the Creator do when His masterpieces rebelled? He searched for them and called out, "Adam, where were you?" We know perfectly well that the Father knew where Adam was. He wanted Adam to realize where he was, to come clean and be honest. I am willing to say that this is probably the number one reason people don't come to God—they are hiding things and hiding themselves and they are afraid on several levels.

Today, the Father is calling out to all of us, "Where are you?" He's asking, "Why are you hiding? What are you trying to cover up? I see you anyway." He wants you to be honest with yourself about where *you* are, because inside the question "Where are you?" is your "Why?" To Adam it's, "I told you to cultivate and create and have dominion. I told you to be like Me—God in the garden, but you let the serpent sneak around the garden." Adam was supposed to be the one who cut the enemy off from paradise.

THE VOICE OF LOVE

When the Father asked, "Where are you?" it wasn't a probe of interrogation but a beckoning voice of love and affection. Actually, it was the voice of *affirmation*. Hear what I'm not saying. I'm not saying God approved of Adam's sin. In no way was God affirming Adam's sin. Sin had to be dealt with, and it was. The Father was *affirming* Adam's existence, letting him know that there was still room for the relationship to be restored. What the Father does is *affirm* your existence, that you were created in His image. Personally, He did it for me, yet He never approved of my sin. Adam got kicked out of the garden because of his disobedience. Because he's out, so are his descendants. That's us. "Wherefore, as by one man sin entered into the world, and death by sin; and so death passed upon all men, for that all have sinned" (Rom. 5:12).

Affirmation from the Father does not disregard our rebellion and fallen natures. What it does say is, "I *am* still here regardless of what you've done. I've made a way for our relationship to be restored because I'm the only source of your existence." The Father gave Adam verbal support through a question, "Where are you?" He was telling Adam, "I'm looking for you. You tore up the whole universe and destroyed what I've created in My relationship with humanity, but I want you back because you belong to me." That's amazing love. That's amazing acceptance with verbal and emotional support at your lowest state. That's when you know you're experiencing *affirmation*. Religion says, "You messed up. Don't tell Dad!" Jesus says, "You messed up. Tell My Father!" Religion wants you to do stuff to try and redeem yourself. Jesus wants you to know what He's already done to redeem you. There was a price that had to be paid. It cost something. First, it was animals. An animal had to be sacrificed to cover Adam with its blood to atone for his sin. The sacrifice didn't take away Adam's sin; it only covered it until the perfect sacrifice of the Lamb would come and cleanse sin. "The next day John saw Jesus coming toward him, and said, 'Behold! The Lamb of God who takes away the sin of the world!'" (John 1:29).

Adam got the benefit of a sacrifice, which *affirmed* his humanity and brought him back into a relationship with divinity. All-knowing and outside of time, seeing the beginning from the end, God knew being in a relationship with mankind would mean unspeakable joy but also great pain. Yet He thought love was worth it. For God it wasn't a risk because He knew all things. Love was worth what He knew was coming, pain and suffering to make a way for us back to Him. Everlasting life begins with being restored to a love relationship with the One who kissed us with His breath. God's love motivates His compassion and mercy. His love brings transformation. Salvation is based on God's fervent love and mercy, not our worthiness. "For we ourselves were also once foolish, disobedient, deceived, serving various lusts and pleasures, living in malice and envy, hateful and hating one another. But when the kindness and the love of God our Savior toward man appeared, not by works of righteousness which we have done, but according to His mercy He saved us, through the washing of regeneration and renewing of the Holy Spirit, whom He poured out on us abundantly through Jesus Christ our Savior" (Titus 3:3–6).

As we have established, God is love, and love can't *not* express itself. You may have children, as I do. We put them in the world despite knowing it had a lot of problems. And even when they fall off the tricycle, we put them back up on it. We knew they would fall. We knew they wouldn't come out driving cars and making perfect decisions, but we already had a plan to pick them up. Love will always sacrifice and do whatever it takes to restore when there is a breach in the relationship. The Father knows the end from the beginning. I can only imagine the beauty of the end, which allows Him to endure the in-between. The Father is going to bring me back to that moment at the table, and I'm going to live there in His presence.

FRIENDS IN LOW PLACES

"And the Word became flesh and dwelt among us" (John 1:14). Jesus was the Word made flesh. He also gave up His reputation, allowing the very people He loved to believe lies about Him. And lest we forget His suffering, horrible, horrific, painful, suffering. At any moment He could have stopped it all. When that rock-jagged and lead-tipped whip came across His back, He could have ended it all. When the spikes were hammered straight through the bones of his feet and wrists, He could have ended it all. "But [Jesus] made Himself of no reputation, taking the form of a bondservant, and coming in the likeness of men. And being found in appearance as a man, He humbled Himself and became obedient to the point of death, even the death of the cross" (Phil. 2:7–8). Jesus became the perfect sacrifice to affirm us.

To be affirmed by the Father means He's come into our low places to meet us there. Even those successful and wealthy and great in the world's eyes have low places where they are hiding. He wants to meet you there in your secret heart. "Mind not high things," penned Paul, "but condescend [stoop] to men of low estate. Be not wise in your own conceits" (Rom. 12:16). This should be of great comfort to us. Whether we realize it or not, we are all people of low estate in some form or fashion, and He lowered Himself to get us. The Father *affirms* us at rock bottom, so we should affirm others in their lowliness. He *affirms* us even when our earthly fathers didn't. We weren't made to carry anger and fear, shame and guilt. We were made to carry peace, restoration and freedom. "I don't approve what you did, but I affirm your existence because you are Mine, you came from Me and you belong to me." The Father was there for Adam and Eve at their lowest state. We matter to Him to the point that He wants the relationship with us we were made for. So he sacrificed the animal to get them back temporarily until the Son was sacrificed to make the relationship permanent. He affirmed their existence, not their behavior.

ISRAEL, OUR EXAMPLE

This was evident in God's dealings with Israel, His chosen people, which was a shadow of the New Covenant through

Jesus. The light by day and fire by night and provision for every need in the wilderness was God's affirmation. Like God uses us today as vessels of the Holy Spirit, God chose Israel to be the people that He would accomplish His plan of redemption and reveal Himself through. But just like Adam, Israel consistently rebelled, and the Father consistently loved them back home to Him. When Israel was enslaved in Egypt for four hundred years under Pharaoh, their deliverance was not based on their behavior. God affirmed their existence. As His beloved, He wanted to make a way for them out of their rebellion in bondage to be restored to a relationship with Him. After hearing their cries for deliverance, He sent Moses. And through Moses to Pharaoh, God systematically destroyed all the idols that the people had begun to see and experience in Egypt as gods.

When Pharaoh still resisted and refused to let Israel go, the Lord took action to prepare the people for the sacrifice that it was going to cost to set them free. Something had to die, just as in the garden, so they didn't have to. It was in their rebellion that the Lord said, "I'm going to let the one who held you in bondage pay the price for you to get *free* with the firstborn sons." But when the blood of the lambs went on the doorposts, that was their *salvation*. This is their exodus story. Their exit started with blood. And that night as the death angel passed over their houses, they were preparing to make haste in the place where they had lived for however long before the blood, as imperfect slaves, in bondage. It was the blood that set them apart to be restored into a relationship with the Creator. Even when they were still in bondage, He was setting them free.

Israel is being saved in their bondage. And His *affirmation* was that "I'm making a way to let you know you belong to Me, to let you know I see you, no matter how dark it is, and to let you know I am near." He revealed His presence by the parting of the Red Sea, with a cloud over them to protect from the scorching sun and heat in the desert. Cloud by day, fire by night. And when they came out rich with all the goods from Egypt, all the wealth, the clothing, the Father was basically saying, "I'm paying you for your labors. I'm going to restore everything that was taken from you so that when we go out into the wilderness, I can be with you again. I told Moses to build a tabernacle because I want to be with him and you. I want to come down." It was always about the relationship, their worship, His presence. "Let My people go that they might worship Me. Not work for Me, worship Me. Get to know Me, be with Me and Me with them." We see His *affirmation* of their existence while they were in bondage. And Moses said to God, "If your Presence does not go with us, do not send us up from here" (Exod. 33:15).

That's the way the Father wants us to live, with His presence going with us through life. The absence of an earthly father giving us affirmation, though needed, does not hinder us from receiving the affirmation from heaven, which is what we've needed. It's not a loss, because the Father in heaven sent His Son.

CHAPTER 20

THE THIRD A: AGREEMENT

One of the things that earthly fathers are supposed to do is set a standard for how we function in healthy ways as young men or young women, and then grow up into maturity. Unfortunately, this standard is woefully lacking in today's culture of fatherlessness. It's tragic because when there is no standard, or value system, we make up our own, and usually it's based on whatever our group's values are or what's convenient when under pressure. We reason that it's OK to maybe cheat a little in certain situations if *not* cheating will cause me trouble or pain. If lying will help me get ahead, then why not? However, if I've been trained in values, if my father lived with integrity, there's a high chance that I'll actually adopt his standards.

Agreement is about what I choose to agree with in my beliefs and in my value system. Where there's no father, a vacuum is created in that area. There is a void in knowing what to believe and how to behave. In that case I take my values from the culture, or whatever my worldview dictates. I might even look into horoscopes. Years ago I used to read under my sign to see what was going to happen in my life. Because I had no spiritual values, I had no way of knowing what meaning and purpose was. When it came to sports, my value was whatever the coaches said and my teammates did. When it came to relationships, my value was what my friends thought and what my flesh wanted.

MODEL MAN

A young student asked Karl Barth to share the most significant theological truth he had discovered in all his years of study. Barth, one of the most prolific theologians of the twentieth century, wrote approximately sixty volumes of commentaries and theological studies. This brilliant man whom many call the most important theologian of modern times thought for a moment, smiled, and said, "Jesus loves me, this I know, for the Bible tells me so."

Nothing, absolutely nothing, can separate us from God's love. "Who shall separate us from the love of Christ? Shall trouble or hardship or persecution or famine or nakedness or danger or sword? As it is written: 'For your sake we face death all day long; we are considered as sheep to be slaughtered.' No, in all these things we are more than conquerors through him who loved us. For I am convinced that neither death nor life, neither angels nor demons, neither the present nor the future, nor any powers, neither height nor depth, nor anything else in all creation, will be able to separate us from the love of God that is in Christ Jesus our Lord!" (Rom. 8:35-39)

Agreement equates to friendship with Jesus, who is Lord. John 15 calls us friends: mental, emotional, and spiritual harmony regarding beliefs and behaviors. Love requires relationship, not rulership, where what you say, think, or feel doesn't matter. Love is a dynamic force or presence that naturally seeks expression. Simply put, love loves! And in order to do that, there must be an object of that love, or it is incomplete. Receive and agree with the gift of His peace. Receive and agree with the gift of His joy. Receive and offer the gift of His love. Forgiveness is something you experience personally. Then, offer it to others daily to remind yourself that as a family you belong to the Lord Jesus and that He belongs to you. This allows you to agree that the way you speak to others, the way you treat others, is the way you are treating Jesus because each of us has been made in the image of God. He is the One who feels the pain the most for how you treat others. He also feels joy the most for how you love others.

Our relationship with God is an intimate one. There is a sacred knowledge and expression that takes place. To know Him intimately is to open the door for revelation and agreement. It brings change, or transformation—change of essence, expression, behavior, desires, identity, and security. The bond is so strong that God says a nursing mother may abandon her child, but He will never abandon us. "Can a mother forget the baby at her breast and have no compassion on the child she has borne? Though she may forget, I will not forget you! See, I have engraved you on the palms of my hands; your walls are ever before me" (Isa. 49:15–16).

When we reflect upon the intensity of our relationship with God, self-doubt often arises. Can we keep our end of the bargain? Our relationship with God, however, is not the sum of our activity directed toward Him but the intensity of our *agreement* in the relationship with Him. Our love is expressed through our devotion to Him, our obedience to His wishes, and our attitudes toward His will and best desires for us. We love God because He loved us first, enabling us to respond properly to His love. "This is how God showed his love among us: He sent his one and only Son into the world that we *might live through him*. This is love: not that we loved God, but that he loved us and sent his Son as an atoning sacrifice for our sins" (1 John 4:9-10, emphasis added)

When you look at agreement, Jesus was the utmost model of what functional humanity should look like as being made in the image of God. "I can only do what I see My Father doing," He said, "I can only say what I hear my Father saying" (John

5:19; 12:49, my paraphrase). Jesus was an exemplar in that He did what the Father directed, but He also modeled how we are at times called to stand alone based on our values, often in the face of ridicule, suffering, and an immoral culture. Jesus was empowered to do so because He knew who He was and to whom He belonged.

In this world ravaged by fatherlessness, one of the many fallouts is the inability of young men and women to step away from the culture to stand and be that one out of one hundred thousand to be a person of God. Knowing *who* they are and to *whom* they belong enables a person to do that. If you have been raised by a faithful father with strong values who stood up for them, you will likely do so. If you belong to the Father with His *ruach*, breath, inside you, instilling His values, you will be empowered to stand. Sometimes standing with the Father's values means taking a stand against the world's.

The Lord brought the children of Israel out of the wilderness into an agreement with His will. The problem was the children of Israel, even when they agreed with God, saw their fathers adapt to life in Egypt so long that they became so rooted in the lifestyle of Egypt. They were trying to hold on to the covenant promises of God to Abraham while holding on to the Egyptian world even though they were slaves. They had a faith, but it was being suffocated. God finally brought them out, and they ended up in the wilderness after seeing the power of God judge Egypt. God miraculously parted the Red Sea and provided for them; even so, they still agreed with the disobedience. The beliefs of their fathers affected their behavior in the wilderness. The bulk of the children of Israel were not interested in a relationship with God. They only agreed as long as He was doing miracles the way they wanted. When the children of Israel murmured and complained against Moses after He did wonders for them, the Father took it personally as a complaint against Him (Num. 14:1–26, 31–45). Because of the lack of agreement in the relationship when God wasn't performing miracles as they wanted, Israel fell out of agreement with Him and came into agreement with their fathers. There is an agreement that is necessary to experience God's purposes in our lives. Agreement is to know what to align with and what not to align with. It is key, and is the bridge between belief and behavior.

Saying Yes Is Saying No

When you care what people think more than anything else, it means you're bound. When I seek to please people, I cease to be a servant of God. I can't do both. I have to choose which relationship is the most important in my life. If I'm going to embrace and live by what is most important, I can't focus on what people think. When I went to the altar and said yes to Le'Chelle and put a ring on her finger, it yelled out, "No!" to all other woman to not even think of coming my way. The answer is no because of the yes to belonging to someone else. Similarly, when we said yes to the One who created us, it shouted, "No!" to the world. His values became ours to understand and cultivate. If your earthly father fell short and left a void of values, they are restored through the Son by the heavenly Father. He gave us His Word as a guide to know what to agree with. "Your word is a lamp to my feet," wrote David, "and a light to my path" (Ps. 119:105).

AS WE ARE IN AN INTIMATE RELATIONSHIP WITH THE FATHER, SIMPLY BEING WHO HE CREATED US TO BE, WALKING IN AGREEMENT WITH HIS VALUES, HE BEGINS TO CONFORM US TO HIS IMAGE.

Agreeing with the One who loves you and affirms you is a game changer. It's the key to how you behave. After the children of Israel were affirmed in their existence and restored in relationship, what did the Father do? He gave them laws. The laws were not to make them miserable but to protect and free them. He was telling His chosen people, "You can agree with this. This is what's going to govern our relationship. This is going to govern your restoration and prosperity, your identity, and release you into the promises that I have for you. This is going to release you to bear witness of My existence in the whole world."

Jesus finished Israel's story, and ours. At the cross we find our Exodus with His blood over the doorpost of our lives. He brings us out of our Egypt and into the freedom of a promised life, not a promised land. Then, we have His Word to determine whether we want to live in agreement with His values. They are divine and make Him the most important relationship of our lives.

As we are in an intimate relationship with the Father, simply being who He created us to be, walking in agreement with His values, He begins to conform us to His image while we're learning to walk in His love. Out of this love relationship He gives us assignments to partner with Him, as He gave Adam. Our answer is yes to Him and no to the enemy that would stop us. We *agree* because we are loved and know the One who is greater moves through us. *Agreement* is the bridge that moves you from a spiritual experience to the solid lifestyle aligning with the One who gave you that experience.

CHAPTER 21

THE FOURTH A: ACCOUNTABILITY

"So then each of us shall give account of himself to God" (Rom. 14:12). "Nothing in all creation is hidden from God's sight. Everything is uncovered and laid bare before the eyes of him to whom we must give account" (Heb. 4:13).

As new creations in Christ, we have been spared from the penalty of eternal death, but all of us will still give an account of our lives and how we've responded and come into agreement with our new identity. "Therefore, if anyone is in Christ, the new creation has come: The old has gone, the new is here!" (2 Cor. 5:17).

Accountability is a relationship that requires a response for responsibilities. When Adam and Eve were put out of the garden and God asked, "Where are you?" He was affirming them yet holding them accountable. He does the same for us. The Father is telling us, "You know who I am. You know what to believe, and your behavior has disagreed with the way I made you and the purpose I made you for." Adam and Eve were able to eat from every tree except the tree of the knowledge of good and evil because if they did, they would die. Was there a moment in your life when your father held you accountable for a certain kind of behavior? That is what good fathers are supposed to do. As the Father's standard bearers, being accountable to Him will ensure that we do not misrepresent Him during our time on this earth.

In Deuteronomy 7:9–16 the Lord shows Israel His blessings and curses and tells them to choose blessings. The Lord gave His provision, promises, and presence to Israel in the wilderness on their way to the promised land, but they had to choose. So do we. Then, when Joshua was finally leading them into the promised land, he told them, "Choose for yourselves this day whom you will serve, whether the gods which your fathers served that were on the other side of the River, or the gods of the Amorites, in whose land you dwell. But as for me and my house, we will serve the Lord" (Josh. 24:15).

With *accountability* comes a choice. We choose how we are going to behave. You have responsibilities that help you grow and be effective. Sure, there are things the Father unconditionally gives us. He gave Israel land and promises. He gave Adam a garden. He gives His righteousness to us as a gift. He did all these things. However, in order to actually cultivate, create, multiply, and deepen our relationship with the Father as well as be a blessing to the world, we must take responsibility.

Accountability is a story about a group of kids who went to play a soccer game one Saturday morning. To their surprise, when they arrived, there were no referees, and the field wasn't marked with lines. After waiting for some time, the parents agreed to let the kids go ahead and play. It was all fun and games to begin with. Then, all of a sudden, kids started yelling and crying because they were getting kicked. Fouling was going on. There was nothing to show when the ball was out of bounds. Parents and the kids were claiming cheating, but there was no one to call the penalties. What was supposed to be fun had become frustrating.

IN ORDER TO ACTUALLY CULTIVATE, CREATE, MULTIPLY, AND DEEPEN OUR RELATIONSHIP WITH THE FATHER AS WELL AS BE A BLESSING TO THE WORLD, WE MUST TAKE RESPONSIBILITY.

After a while, the referee and the maintenance man showed up. They paused the game while the maintenance man lined the field. Then, the referee called the players back onto the field to play. Now they could tell when the ball was out of bounds. They could tell when someone scored, and they called penalties. The whole game was set in order. When the referee with the authority had arrived and the boundaries were clearly drawn, they were free to play and unleash their full potential. Freedom is not the ability to run wild and do whatever you want. Freedom is the ability to do what you should do.

Those two trees God planted in the garden represented the two ways man can choose to live. The tree of life represented dependence upon God. The tree of the knowledge of good and evil represented independence from God. The Father gave the commandment to Adam, "Do not eat from the tree of the knowledge of good and evil." Most people focus on that, but what did God tell him before giving that command? "You are free to eat from any tree in the garden" (Gen. 2:16). God the Father gave Adam permission for freedom before He ever gave him restrictions. The father is looking to free us, while Satan is looking to deceive us into thinking our Creator wants to enslave us. The actuality is we will never be truly at liberty until we are in a relationship with the Father and living inside His boundaries for our freedom. You can eat from any other trees and stay free.

Adam and Eve were set. They had it all with everything to lose. But look at how cunningly the enemy works. "God didn't really mean that. Go ahead, do what you want. There's so much more out there. God just wants to spoil your fun. You can be like Him" (Gen. 3:1–6, my paraphrase). The enemy will take the one thing you can't have and deceive you into believing that's the one thing that's going to satisfy you. He does this while causing you to miss all the true freedom and life you can have.

But the Father was protecting and providing within safe boundaries. Just look at the brutal reality that resulted from Adam's and Eve's choices. Living inside the garden, they experienced magnificent paradise, perfect weather, fullness of food and pleasure, and purpose while walking in God's ever-enveloping presence. Outside the garden they got a false freedom attached to pain, thorns, insecurity, shame, and a host of other consequences of sin.

Now, there is certainly pleasure in sin. Sin is fun and gratifies the flesh. People who say sin is not fun are lying. The catch is, it's fun for a season, and then it starts making you pay. The popular saying goes, "Sin will take you further than you want to go, keep you longer than you want to stay, and cost you more than you want to pay." The Bible says, Moses chose "to suffer affliction with the people of God than to enjoy the passing pleasures of sin" (Heb. 11:25). Sin has its pleasures, to be sure, but they always pass. Bottom line: "The wages of sin is death" (Rom. 6:23). It will always kill you. That's what the enemy doesn't want you to know. That's what your flesh wants you to ignore.

Accountability is Jesus saying to the disciples, "Whoever desires to save his life will lose it, but whoever loses his life for My sake will find it" (Matt. 16:25). What good would it be for someone to eat from the tree of the knowledge of good and evil and be independent from the Father, doing their own thing, trying to play soccer with no lines and no referees? It's chaos. What good would it be for you to do whatever you want and gain the whole world if you forfeit your authentic self? What can anyone give in exchange for their soul? It's sobering to consider how many people have sold their souls to Satan and his world system in the name of pleasure. Two things are absolute facts: (1) We are all going to die, some sooner than later, and (2) we *will* stand before God the Father to give an account for what we have done. We will be held accountable. Thank God for Jesus.

But how do I live in accountability when my old nature is screaming to rebel? I live in accountability through friendship with Jesus. "I have called you friends, for everything that I learned from my Father I have made known to you" (John 15:15). Jesus wants to make everything about the Father known to us, and that knowledge comes through abiding in Him through deep friendship. This happens practically by feeding on His Word. Jesus cut through any confusion and said, "Man doesn't live by bread alone, but by every word that proceeds out of the mouth of God," (Matt. 4:4, my paraphrase). I love how Jesus used the metaphor of what food does for our body, the Word does for our spirit. I need the bread of life to stay alive and be healthy spiritually.

When you feed on the Word of God, the hungrier you become, which means the more you eat and the stronger you become. There is no word from God without power. The Father Himself said, "My word...shall not return to Me void, but it shall accomplish what I please, and it shall prosper in the thing for which I sent it" (Isa. 55:11). "So then faith comes by hearing, and hearing by the word of God" (Rom. 10:17). The more word, the more faith, the more power. The only way we can be empowered to be accountable and live in agreement with what the Father wants to do in and through us is by filling our minds and spirits with His Word and then choosing to live and play the game of life inside His prescribed boundaries.

The Father always has our best interest in mind, more so than we do. The boundaries are that you gave up your own life, but by losing it, you gain true life. There's a responsibility, a response, a bonus that comes when you know that your identity is "You are loved and affirmed." Now, I agree with the values of this new life and have the responsibility to give an *account* for that in my lifestyle. Accountability is about responding to the Father and aligning our values with His.

CHAPTER 22

THE FIFTH A: ACCESS

Our final principle of the Five A's is *access* to the Father. This is about eternal life. Ideally, our earthly fathers instilled in us a measure of acceptance, affirmation, agreement, and accountability. If they were able to impart these principles to us and speak them into our lives, they would be setting the stage for us to trust Jesus as the Savior of our lives and the One who introduces us to the Father. An earthly father should be a door. or gateway, of access to God the Father for His children to follow. The problem is many, many, many people, millions of people, when looking at their earthly father, see a wall, not a door, and certainly not a gateway. They see a period, not a comma. Their father has negatively defined them, which distorts their view of God. When you mention God as a loving Father, they cringe.

The Five A's break this cycle of shame and yoke of burden of *not* having something that my earthly father was supposed to give me. Because of Jesus my access to the Father doesn't have to be hindered due to the pain and rejection from my earthly father. I don't have to be hopeless anymore. I don't have to be caught up in addiction. I don't have to feel abandoned, lost, angry, or bitter. I don't have to feel like an orphan, questioning and wondering, "Am I worth anything?"

Jesus came as a substitute for what your earthly father didn't give you—and that includes access to the Father. "Through him, we both have access to the Father by one Spirit" (Eph. 28:4). Earthly fathers are the sources of our lives here on earth that come to an end, but the heavenly Father is the source of eternal life that never ends. Jesus is exposing us to access to the Father through the great sacrifice of His love.

WALKING THROUGH WALLS

For myself, I had erected high, thick walls of protection all around me. Jesus, however, walked right through them as He did for the disciples when they were locked in a room after His resurrection. Jesus made a door where there was none. He opened a gateway to new life. Jesus was the access point between the disciples and the Father—and between me and the Father. Now I have access to eternal life, and the experience has changed my human condition. It also has changed my purpose. I, one who had no access, have become an access point to the Father to those who are fatherless so they too can be *fatherless no more.*

In order to step into this freedom, however, one has to be willing to acknowledge that they are in need. Rebellion says, "I don't need a father." False identity says, "I don't need a father." Your brokenness, though, is evidence that you do need a father, *the* Father. And it's when we've experienced Him that our mess becomes a masterpiece in the hands of the master sculptor.

We need freedom from the strongholds and chains that have us locked up, from sin patterns, habits, and behaviors that can't be broken without the power of God. Adam made us orphans, but Jesus said, "I will not leave you as orphans." He came to make us *fatherless no more.* However, in order to access all that we've been talking about, turn the key to the prison door and break the effects of fatherlessness, there are five access points that help us establish the Five A's. They are:

1) *Acknowledge* all these things are true. Admit that you needed a father.

2) *Confess* how it made you feel to not be fathered. I have to be willing to confess that I have issues. This is something no one wants to admit, but it's needful. No one wants to say that they're empty, they're fearful, they're angry and feel rejected and directionless. I can't tell you how many times I stood up at a podium at some banquet to receive an award—All American, All State, Athlete of the Year, Lineman of the Year. On the outside I looked all together, yet there would be churning inside of me that I would never want my coaches or mom or anyone to know about. But when Jesus walked through my wall and showed me the Father, all this pain came exploding out of me. I realized my need, but I didn't know how to process what was happening. Jesus, through His love and grace, began giving me these Five A's by revelation. They can help you if you haven't had that encounter as I did. The process can help you humble yourself and say, "I confess, I treat women a certain way because of the absence of a father's voice. Because of that absence, I treat myself a certain way. The pain is real. My desire for money and sex came from the absence of values." I have to acknowledge these things before I can begin finding healing.

3) *Forgive* my father, because if I don't, I'm living in a prison that is holding me in bondage. I'm also punishing those around me when I'm living out of my pain. If you had, or have, a good father, you may not feel you're in prison. Still, you're bound to simply what your father was able to give you, and you're missing the freedom that comes only from the Father. The problem sometimes with good fathers who don't point people to the Father is that they become idols. Yes, he was a gift to you, but he wasn't your God. There's no freedom when we don't understand that the pain of our lives is rooted in our

fatherlessness from the Father. We blame circumstances, that job, this or that, when really the way I act toward people, and the way I respond to them, reveals that I have a father wound. Holding on to unforgiveness and bitterness is almost like going to a jail cell. A jail cell can be on Wall Street. It can be at any corporate office, a private country club, or Rikers Island Correctional Facility. Everywhere you go, you are affected by this fatherlessness that has left you empty and not knowing who you are. It's all you've ever known—but here comes Jesus. He walks right through the walls of your cell and taps you on the shoulder. He says, "You can let those bars go. I've opened a door of access for you. I've made a new way out, but it's through Me. I want to forgive you so you can forgive and be free." And you have a sense of hope because His presence is so real. It's always soothing. It's so affirming. It's everything you agree with.

4) *Release* your father from your heart because forgiveness stops the pain. "I'm going to relinquish the way I want to punish this person or make them pay for what they didn't give me. I realize they were not equipped to give me what they didn't know. I'm going to relieve myself from them. I forgive them." Forgiveness is a big step to stopping pain. Releasing starts the healing, or you will become what you don't release. Has somebody ever said to you, "You're just like your dad"? If you have father wounds, those words cut through to your core. You wanted nothing to do with that, yet because you didn't forgive him and let him go, you're becoming that in a different version.

Now, Jesus is standing in the cell with outstretched arms, waiting. Releasing is turning away from all your offense and saying, "I'm going to walk with You, Jesus. I'm going to walk into the freedom that only You can give me." And there's a certain fear in doing that, because at the least, we don't know how to live without this discomfort, this dis-ease and confusion in the soul. Sometimes the hurting parts of us are the most comforting parts of us. We can control it by being controlled by it, which is quite an odd paradox.

YOU CAN SEE THAT BECAUSE I'VE BEEN FATHERED BY HIM, HE MADE ME WHAT I NEVER THOUGHT, AN ACCESS POINT.

At this point, you have a decision to make. Cling to Jesus, the exact representation of the Father, with the hands you use to let go of your bars so that you can grip with every ounce of your being who He is and what He has to offer.

5) *Receive.* Once you forgive and release, then repent and receive. Repent of the bitterness and unforgiveness. Repent of the rebellion and lust, trust Christ, and then believe that through forgiveness of sin and new life, there will be guidance. "But when he, the Spirit of truth, comes," promised Jesus, "he will guide you into all the truth. He will not speak on his own; he will speak only what he hears, and he will tell you what is yet to come. He will glorify me because it is from me that he will receive what he will make known to you. All that belongs to the Father is mine. That is why I said the Spirit will receive from me what he will make known to you" (John 16:13–15). When you receive the Father's love through the Son, you begin walking a defined life in the Spirit that never ends. There's forgiveness and fruitfulness. Because you now "have peace with God [the Father] through our Lord Jesus Christ" (Rom. 5:1), your life exists in alignment with Him, and as an added bonus, you get to become an access point for others! This is what personally happened to me. Not only has He fathered me through all the pains and mistakes and everything, but He has also fathered me while I father my children and love my wife. The

Father has allowed me to be a father to people who are not my biological children. And you can see that because I've been fathered by Him, He made me what I never thought, an access point. Thank you, Lord. He made me what I never was before. When I ponder the reality of how life-changing this one experience of knowing the father is, there's nothing more liberating. This is what the Father wants to do for you.

CONCLUSION

COMING TO YOUR SENSES

The most powerful thing that can happen to a human being is that they come to their senses. That's what happened to me. I was living life my way, making it up as I went. And then I came to my senses and realized, after the Word and the light coming to me, I was dying out here. I was supposed to be having all this fun, but instead I was empty, locked in that prison of false freedom. The way to the Father was made through the Son, Jesus, to come home, to be safe, to find a place to belong, to be covered, to be secure. Religion wants you to pay for your mistakes, but the Father, if He sees us coming back, comes running and lets everybody know, "She's my daughter. He's my son. They belong to me!" This is the Father who rescued me. This is the Father who's inviting every man, woman, guy, baby's mama, baby's daddy, executive, musician, athlete, whomever, to have their identity and everything else transformed. When I turned, He covered me with His love, and it changed everything. When I stayed close to Him, He brought me home. The Father didn't make me a servant. He didn't let anybody condemn me.

Take the story of the prodigal son. The darkness made perfect sense to him. "I'm not going to wait on you, Dad. Give me what's mine, now. I have a plan." In that ancient culture those words and actions were like saying, "Dad, you're dead to me. You don't matter." It was *fatherless no more* in reverse. "What matters to me is what I want the world to see about me. I got this, Dad. I'm riding in the wind with the top down, speakers banging with all the latest music. I got the girls. I got the party because I got money." It made perfect sense to him. But he lost his soul when he left his Father, and he was living in darkness when it ran its course.

You know the rest of the story. It's recorded in Luke chapter 15. The NIV says he "squandered" and "began to be in need" (vv. 13–14). Finding ourselves in need, emotionally or physically, is not the worst thing that could happen to us. In fact, it can be the best thing. After it got so bad for the prodigal and he was faced with eating with the pigs, the Bible says, "He came to his senses" (v. 17). Nothing will wake you up like eating with the pigs. It jolted him to his senses. God uses the darkness to push us toward the light. So what did he do? He thought about what he gave up. He thought about how good his father was and how much different life was under his father's roof, living in the boundaries, the acceptance, the affirmation, the agreement, the account-ability, and the access to the Father. And he said, "It can't compare with what I settled for. I gave up what my father was providing for me for what I wanted to do for myself." He turned toward home. And the cool part is, as the prodigal son was stumbling and fumbling his way home, the father saw him in the distance. He'd been watching and waiting. And then, the prodigal watched as his father started running toward him. You know why? First, because the father loved his son simply for who he was, even in his rebellion and failure. Secondly, because the father knew that in first-cen-tury culture, if you ever dishonored your father, the villagers had a right to punish by stoning. The father knew his boy was headed for trouble coming back home after disowning and disrespecting him. But what did his father do? He ran out to meet him, to cover him from the condemnation that he deserved. And also, in the first century it was considered undignified for Jewish men to run. When they did, it looked as if they had lost control. But this father ran. He got undignified and made himself lesser so his son could become greater. He put himself down to lift his son up. He covered his son to let everyone know, "I approve of his repentance. I approve of him coming to his senses and realizing what life in light looks like from a place of death." The son was genuinely repentant and felt unworthy. However, the father didn't care about the past. All he cared about is his son was back home with him. Let the celebration begin. "But the father said to his servants, 'Quick! Bring the best robe and put it on him. Put a ring on his finger and sandals on his feet. Bring the fattened calf and kill it. Let's have a feast and celebrate. For this son of mine was dead and is alive again; he was lost and is found.' So they began to celebrate" (Luke 15:22–24).

Living in spiritual separation is death, but when you come to your senses, you have a chance to be restored back to life. The son was thinking he'd just be a servant, but the father was saying, "I'm giving you the full rights of sonship and the blessing of my authority and endorsement on your life."

Coming to your senses and coming back home to the Father is the best thing that could happen to you. Then, you can begin walking in the light for the rest of your life. The Father's life is all yours. If you've got Him, you have everything.

Let me ask you this: What would it do to a child if they knew they were pleasing to their father? What would it do to young ladies and men who've gone sideways morally because they're looking to satisfy that hole in their soul in the shape of their dad, who didn't come to secure them and make them feel as if they belong, and they were understood, and they were cared for? That's available to everyone who's willing to humble themselves and say, "I don't feel I belong. I actually know the hole in my soul; I feel the emptiness. I can look back at my life, and say I have been defined by the wrong things." There's a lot of insecurity in the world because we haven't had the right love, the right identity, the right relationship to impact us.

HOLE IN THE SOUL

The whole world is in an identity crisis. We see violence, wars, famine, and more because the crisis of not knowing who they are can cause offense and a negative impact on those around them. Hurt people hurt people. They don't know that they've been created for more than fear, more than anger. Confusion exists when I have no idea who I am. Sadly, this is the baseline of the human condition.

I think every human being has a sense of something beyond them. That's why people create religions. They know they didn't originate life, that they came from somewhere, life came from somewhere. They may have different phrasing philosophies and ideas about what that is. But ultimately, I believe that the God who created us put a longing for eternity in our hearts (Eccles. 3:11). He put a desire for something greater and deeper inside us. I once heard this said: "God whispers in the womb of every mother to a child, that 'there is a man waiting for you, to take care of you, to love you, to protect you, to provide for you.' There is a desire for that from every child when they're born into this world. If that man is not there, there's a wound not easily healed or satisfied. If it doesn't get healed or satisfied, there's a hole in our soul in the shape of our dad. There's a hole in our soul that wants to be defined, that wants to belong, that wants to know what to believe and not have to make it up on our own but be shaped by the people responsible for bringing us into this world."

It's like the story of the older gentleman who happened upon a young boy who was flying a kite. The kite was so high that it was caught in the clouds, and this older gentleman went to the boy and asked, "What are you doing?"

"I'm flying a kite," the boy replied.

"What? I don't see a kite," the man said.

"You don't have to see it," said the boy. "But I know it exists."

"How do you know?"

"Because I feel its tug."

There was a string attached to the kite. The kid knew the kite existed even though it was beyond the clouds. I think that's what exists inside us. We may not see the Father, but we feel His tug. I felt His tug and, like most people, feel the tug, and you can do what I did—run away, not face it, not deal with it until you come back to that crisis moment where it begins to get louder and more pronounced. The emptiness grows, where you have to ask those questions.

THE FATHER'S DESIRE IS TO EMBRACE US AND OVERFLOW US WITH HIS LOVE WHILE ENLARGING OUR CAPACITY TO RECEIVE HIS LOVE AND GIVE IT TO OTHERS.

My prayer for you, daughters and sons, is that as you have read this book, you will receive this *word from God*, and even if you don't have deep father wounds, the Father will captivate your heart with His outrageous love. The Father's desire is to embrace us and overflow us with His love while enlarging our capacity to receive His love and give it to others. We were created for Him. Our true identity is in Him, and we are enough. Jesus is saying, "I see you. I see what you're doing. You don't know whom you belong to, and you can't help it. But it's OK. I'm not mad at you. I want to free you and bring you home to the Father." What humanity thirsts for more than any-thing is home. You long for a place of belonging, love, inti-macy, togetherness, and wholeness. Actually, it's not just what we thirst for; it's what we were created for.

ACKNOWLEDGMENTS

There is legitimately and honestly not enough room to list all the people who have made an impact on me and on the completion of this book. I know and you know who you are. I appreciate you deeply and look forward to seeing the fruit of how the Father is working through our lives. I do want to say thank you to David Morillo for going the extra mile and walking every single step of this six-year journey with me. To the Orlando World Outreach Church staff, thank you for the impact you have made on my life by the way you love, lead, learn, and lean in to how Jesus is building His church.

I appreciate you, Ma, for showing me how to work hard and to never give up even when it's hard. Don, Mike, Fleda, and Alvin, I am grateful to call you my brothers and sister. The lessons we've learned together have been priceless. For my in-laws, Ryan, Nechelle, Terrie, Gayle, and Mom Varis, thank you for your prayers, for seeds sown, and for believing in this vision. To Christa, Kayla, Karrah, and Shaun, who know me and love me, I adore each of you, and I love you from the deepest part of my heart.

To the love of my life, Le'Chelle, when I think of how much you have loved me, you are an anchor for our family, and you sacrifice to follow everything the Father has called us to, I am overwhelmed by the thought "Where would I be without you?" All I know is life with you is where I want to be for the rest of my days. Thank you, my love, for being you.

ABOUT THE COVER

Choosing the cover for this book was an unexpectedly personal journey. As an author, I learned that the perfect cover must not only reflect the soul of the story but also captivate potential readers and meet the expectations of the genre. While many authors wrestle with this decision, for me it was clear. The cover image, captured by my son Shaun Johnson, holds profound meaning. I didn't know he took the picture as we were having lunch while dropping him off at college. It's much more than just a picture—it's a testament to the life I've lived as a father, a role that resonates with me deeply. I am moved every time I see this photo my son took of me because I've never had the chance to see a picture of my own father. This cover symbolizes a legacy of faith, love, and the powerful bond between father and son because I am fatherless no more.

ENDNOTES

CHAPTER 7

1.   Og Mandino, *The Greatest Salesman in the World* (New York: Frederick Fell, 1968).

CHAPTER 13

1.   Jack Deere, *Surprised by the Voice of God: How God Speaks Today Through Prophecies, Dreams, and Visions* (Grand Rapids, MI: Zondervan, 1996), 321–322.

CHAPTER 17

1.   "Households Without Dads," The DAD University, accessed October 5 2024, https://suitupministries.org/where_are_all_the_dads_; "Influence of Fathers," Prezi, accessed October 5, 2024, https://prezi.com/lwded-rebjnl/influence-of-fathers/.

ABOUT THE AUTHOR

Tim Johnson is a former NFL Super Bowl champion, Sports Illustrated All-Pro, NCAA Football All-American, and Penn State national champion. Previously named National Faith-Based Leader of the Year by the John C. Maxwell Organization, he serves as senior pastor of Orlando World Outreach Church, president of the Orlando Serve Foundation, and founder of the Fatherless No More initiative. Johnson travels the globe speaking to thousands in churches, pro athlete facilities, jails, and prisons. Johnson is husband to Le'Chelle and father to Christa, Kayla, Karrah, and Shaun.